MOSAIC KNITTING

MOSAIC KNITTING

BARBARA G. WALKER

Photography by Werner P. Brodde

Charles Scribner's Sons, New York

Acknowledgments

My deepest gratitude to the following, for their several contributions to this book: to Werner P. Brodde for the infinite patience, goodwill, and expertise that distinguish his beautiful photography; to Beverly Tharp for her skill and kindness in helping to knit samples; to Robert-Peter Aby for his original ideas, shown in six of the band patterns; to my models, Judy Boettger, Andrea and Thomas Brodde, Mary Ann Bucklin, Karen Eschenlauer, Noel Sorvino, Alan and Gordon Walker, and Linda Wood, for their willing assistance; to my editor, Elinor Parker, for her unfailing helpfulness and competence; to Austral Enterprises, Emile Bernat & Sons Company, and the Spinnerin Yarn Company, for materials; and last but not least, to my husband, Gordon N. Walker, for putting up with the seemingly endless clutter of papers and yarn balls that littered all my days and ways.

B. G. W.

TABLE OF CONTENTS

v

INTRODUCTION

Mosaic knitting is a new term in the knitter's vocabulary. It describes a novel development in color-knitting technique and a whole new class of patterns, each different from any pattern that has ever been used before. The term was coined, and the patterns of this class have been invented, by the author of this book. Previous books (*A Second Treasury of Knitting Patterns, Charted Knitting Designs, Sampler Knitting,* and *Barbara Walker's Learn-To-Knit Afghan Book*) also present collections of original mosaic patterns. But the patterns given in this volume are entirely new, unlike any included in previous collections. If you have already enjoyed trying out the easy-knitting, dramatic designs that are created by mosaics, you'll love this new assortment of patterns. If you've never tried mosaic knitting before, you'll find it easy to learn and exciting to use.

Though all mosaic patterns are unique, the basic technique is neither unusual nor excessively demanding. Do you know how to knit a stitch, and how to slip a stitch? That's all you need. If you know these two simplest of all knitting operations, then in fact you already know how to do mosaic knitting. Each fascinating mosaic pattern uses only these two operations, with purling, sometimes, as an occasional option. Despite this extreme simplicity, however, mosaic knitting is quite different from the old method of working designs in color.

In the old method (Fair Isle knitting, which you're accustomed to seeing in Scandinavian-style ski sweaters and the like), the knitter must work with two strands of yarn at once, knitting some stitches with one color and some with another while unused strands are carried across the back of the work or wound on bobbins. Mosaic knitting is *not* like this. In mosaic knitting, the knitter never has to handle more than one strand of yarn at a time. There are no extra lengths on the back of the work to thicken the fabric or make it lumpy, puckered, or uneven—as Fair Isle knitting almost invariably looks when it is done by a beginner. Truly, mosaic knitting is a beginner's paradise. Even a comparatively unskilled knitter can achieve spectacular results without any of the tension problems that plague Fair Isle work.

Mosaic knitting has many other advantages for the beginner. Any mosaic pattern can be worked on any number of stitches, so there's no need to worry about stitch counting and casting on correct multiples for each pattern. Also, all mosaic patterns knit to the same gauge (number of stitches and rows to the inch) as long as yarn and needle sizes remain unchanged. Patterns can be changed at will in the same piece of knitting, without altering the stitch count or the size. You never have to increase or decrease to accommodate a different gauge when passing from one pattern to another. Mosaic knitting makes no special demands on the knitter's materials. It can be worked on needles of any diameter, from zero to enormous, with yarn of any weight from fine two-ply to bulky. Furthermore, mosaic knitting gives you a choice of two basic fabric styles, *garter stitch* or *stockinette stitch*. The same patterns can be used with equal success in both, either, or a combination of them. To make mosaic patterns on a garter-stitch fabric, you knit the wrong-side rows as well as the right-side rows. To make mosaic patterns on a stockinette-stitch fabric, you purl the wrong-side rows. To make a combination, you knit the wrong-side rows of one color, and purl the wrong-side rows of the other color.

Each color, in mosaic knitting, is used for two entire rows at a time, a right-side row followed by a wrong-side row. The other color is not touched until these two rows are finished; it hangs loose at the right-hand edge of the knitting, waiting its turn. To change from one color to the other, you finish a wrong-side row, turn the work around to the right side, drop the strand you've been using on the right side of the work toward you, and pick up the other strand behind it. Then you're ready to work the next two rows. Colors always change after every wrong-side row, so the two-row stripes neatly alternate along the side edge. It's easy to count these stripes, so you always know exactly how many rows have been finished.

Mosaic patterns are formed only by slipping stitches—that is, by passing the stitch from the left needle to the right needle without working it. All slip-stitches, on every row, are slipped in the ordinary way, purlwise. That means that you insert the right-hand needle point into the stitch from behind, as if to purl. For other kinds of patterns one sometimes uses a knitwise slip, by inserting the needle into the stitch from in front; but for mosaic patterns one never does.

Mosaic patterns have another general rule about slipping stitches. When a stitch is slipped, the working yarn is held always to the wrong side of the work. There are no exceptions to this rule. Therefore, if you are working on a right-side row, and consequently facing the right side of the knitting, every slip-stitch is slipped with the yarn held behind the stitch, on the side away from you. This is called slipping with yarn in back, abbreviated "wyib." If you are working on a wrong-side row, and consequently facing the wrong side of the knitting, every slip-stitch is slipped with the yarn held in front of the stitch, on the side toward you. This is called slipping with yarn in front, abbreviated "wyif." When you are working a mosaic pattern in rounds on a circular needle, of course you are always facing the right side of the work; so every slip-stitch, on every round, is slipped with yarn in back.

These basic principles are well known to every knitter who has ever done any pattern incorporating slip-stitches. For such patterns, you've read directions that go something like this: "Row 1 (right side)—K1, * sl 1, k3, sl 2, k5; rep from * , end sl 1, k1." Of course these abbreviations tell you to work right-side Row 1 as follows: knit one stitch, * slip one stitch, knit 3, slip 2, knit 5; repeat over and over from * to the last two stitches of the row, ending slip one, knit one. Directions for mosaic patterns can be written this same way. But in this book the directions are given in a more convenient way: by a graphic chart, which shows you a black-and-white picture of each pattern while telling you how to knit it. After you become accustomed to this, you'll find that charted directions are much easier to read than lines of print. The first chapter, which is entitled "Mosaic Knitting from Charts," will tell you exactly how to use every chart in this book. Go through this section with great care, needles and yarn in hand, and work the example pattern as you go. Then you'll be well prepared to master all the intriguing mosaic patterns, band patterns, design ideas, and delightfully interesting shadow patterns. For dessert, a final chapter will acquaint you with the unusual technique of basketweave knitting and show how mosaic patterns may be applied to it.

Welcome to the colorful world of mosaic knitting. I hope you'll enjoy it.

B. G. W.

Mount Kemble Lake
Morristown, N.J.

MOSAIC KNITTING

Figure 1

Example Pattern (MOSAIC 1)

Multiple of 8 sts plus 3

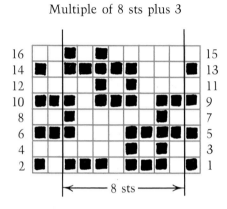

Figure 1. Example Pattern
(Mosaic 1). Above: stockinette-stitch version; below:
garter-stitch version

MOSAIC KNITTING FROM CHARTS

A Step-by-Step, Stitch-by-Stitch Description

To learn to knit any mosaic pattern from a chart, you will make a swatch of a simple little 8-stitch, 16-row example pattern. Look at the chart for this pattern. It tells you immediately that there are 16 rows to be repeated, since the row numbers at the side edges of the chart go up to 16; and it tells you that the pattern is to be worked on a multiple of 8 stitches plus 3 edge stitches. The number of stitches in a single repeat, 8, is printed at the bottom of the chart as well as at the top. Also, the chart shows you a *picture*, in black and white squares which correspond to dark and light stitches, of what the design looks like on the knitted fabric in a single repeat of 8 stitches and 16 rows.

Before you begin to knit, memorize these five basic points about mosaic charts:

1. Each horizontal row of squares on the chart represents *two* rows of knitting, a right-side row and the following wrong-side row. In mosaic knitting, these two rows are alike, and they are both worked with the same strand of yarn. The right-side row, beginning with an odd number at the right-hand edge of the chart, works from right to left, just as the knitting goes. The wrong-side row, shown by an even number at the left-hand edge of the chart *on the same line*, brings the same color back to the right-hand edge of the knitting, where it can be exchanged for the other color.

2. The right-side rows begin at the right-hand edge of the chart with black and white squares alternately. These squares represent the first stitch of each row at the right-hand edge of the knitting. On every right-side row that begins with a black square, you knit all the black stitches, and slip all the white stitches, purlwise, with yarn in back. On every right-side row that begins with a white square, you knit all the white stitches, and slip all the black stitches, purlwise, with yarn in back. Read the preceding two

sentences again! They give you the fundamental principle of charted mosaic knitting.

3. Rows are numbered, and worked, from bottom to top of the chart, just as the knitting goes. Every pattern in this book begins with two rows of the yarn corresponding to the black squares, because Rows 1 and 2 are marked on every chart with a black square at the lower right-hand corner. Therefore, before starting any of these patterns, *always* cast on with the yarn corresponding to the *white* squares, and knit or purl one preliminary row all the way across. After this preliminary row, tie the end of the "black" yarn onto the "white" yarn, close to the needle. Drop the "white" yarn, letting it hang, and use the "black" yarn only to begin the pattern. To start a mosaic pattern on preexisting knitting, first work at least one right-side row and one wrong-side row with "white" yarn.

4. The two vertical lines near the side edges of the chart are repeat lines. They mean the same as "*" in written directions. Outside the repeat lines there are three extra edge stitches, one on the right, two on the left. These edge stitches are worked only at the beginning and end of the row. The actual pattern is contained between the repeat lines, as shown by the stitch number and arrows at the bottom of the chart. So, to work a right-side row, knit the first edge stitch, pass the first (right-hand) repeat line, and work across the row from right to left until you come to the second (left-hand) repeat line; stop, zip back to the first repeat line, and continue the pattern from the first square *inside* this line. Proceed across the row, always reading from right to left between the repeat lines, until you come to the end of your stitches. Then—and only then—pass the second repeat line and work the last two edge stitches.

5. On every wrong-side row of a mosaic pattern, you ignore the chart! Instead of looking at the chart, you look only at the stitches on your needle. If you have just finished a right-side row with black, for instance, your needle will have some black stitches that were knitted on that row and some white stitches that were slipped on that row. To work the wrong-side row, still using black, you knit (or purl) those same black stitches again, and slip those same white stitches again, purlwise, with yarn in *front* (remember that the yarn is held always to the wrong side of the work for slipping stitches). Since each wrong-side row copies the preceding right-side row exactly, you "read" it from the colors of the stitches on your needle instead of from the chart. Just work the stitches of the color that you are holding, and slip the stitches of the other color.

Now let's get down to business, and learn by doing. Take up your needles, and 2 contrasting colors of yarn, light and dark, of the same weight. With the light yarn, cast on 35 stitches. This is a multiple of 8 (32) plus 3, as directed by the example pattern. With the light yarn, purl 1 row. Tie the dark yarn onto the light yarn as described in Point 3, and get ready to work Row 1 with dark yarn, because it begins with a black square on the chart. Place a ruler or card on the chart so that it covers all but the first horizontal row of squares at the bottom, which is the only row you have to see right now.

> Row 1 (right side)—With Dark, k1, * sl 1, k3, sl 1, k3; rep from *, end sl 1, k1.

This is exactly what Row 1 on the chart says. Having knitted the first edge stitch outside the repeat line, you come to a white square, indicating a slip-stitch because you are working on a *black* row. This is followed by three black squares, or three dark knitted stitches; then another white slip-stitch and three more knitted stitches. This brings you to the left-hand repeat line, so you zip back to the first repeat line (*) and continue from there. Because you are working on a right-side row, you'll slip all slip-stitches with yarn in back.

> Row 2 and all other wrong-side rows—With the same color as previous row, purl all the same stitches of that color, knitted on the previous row; slip all the same slip-stitches of the other color, with yarn in front.

This is just what you read in Point 5. Looking at the needle, not the chart, purl all the dark stitches because they are the same color as your working yarn, and slip all the light stitches. At the end of this row, turn the work, drop the dark yarn toward you, pick up the light yarn behind it, and prepare to work Row 3, which begins with a white square. Move the ruler or card up the chart so that it shows you Rows 3 and 4 on the second line.

> Row 3—With Light, k1, * (k1, sl 1) twice, k4; rep from *, end k2.

On this row you are reversing the procedure of Row 1. Because you are using the yarn corresponding to white squares, you *knit* all the stitches shown by white squares and *slip* all the stitches shown by black squares. Notice that the "k4" at the end of the repeat, together with the first "k1" of the next repeat, makes a total of five light stitches knitted consecutively. On the following wrong-side Row 4, you will be purling all the *light* stitches on the needle, because they are the same color as the working yarn, and slipping all the *dark* stitches with yarn in front, according to the direction of Row 2.

Row 5—With Dark, k1, * k4, sl 3, k1; rep from *, end k2.

Having changed colors again and moved the ruler up another line, you see that this black row has 3 white squares together, indicating 3 light slip-stitches. Notice that the "k1" at the end of the repeat, together with the first "k4" of the next repeat, makes a total of 5 dark stitches knitted consecutively.

Row 7—With Light, k1, * k1, sl 1, k5, sl 1; rep from *, end k2.
Row 9—With Dark, k1, * k2, sl 1, k3, sl 1, k1; rep from *, end k2.

You can see that Row 9 is a three-and-one row like Row 1, because the "k1" at the end and the "k2" at the beginning add up to 3 dark knitted stitches.

Row 11—With Light, k1, * k3, sl 1, k1, sl 1, k2; rep from *, end k2.
Row 13—With Dark, k1, * sl 3, k5; rep from *, end sl 1, k1.

The black square at the right-hand edge of Row 13 shows that it is worked with dark yarn; therefore the 3 white squares inside the first repeat line are 3 slip-stitches.

Row 15—With Light, k1, * k5, sl 1, k1, sl 1; rep from *, end k2.
Row 16—See Row 2.
Repeat Rows 1–16.

Now you've gone once through all the pattern rows, and you can see the design taking shape in your knitting, just as it looks on the chart. Go through these pattern rows again, *without* reading the written directions.

Look only at the chart, so you will become accustomed to seeing those squares as stitches and counting them up as you travel across each row.

You have been making a stockinette-stitch type of fabric, because you have been purling the stitches on every wrong-side row. After two or three repeats of the pattern rows, change to a garter-stitch type of fabric by *knitting*, instead of purling, the stitches on wrong-side rows. Everything else remains the same; you still slip the slip-stitches purlwise, with yarn in front, on wrong-side rows. To do this—since the yarn is held in back for knitting the other stitches—remember to bring the yarn forward between the needle points before each slip-stitch, and pass it to the back again after the stitch has been slipped. Continue working several more repeats of the same pattern rows in the garter-stitch style, knitting on the wrong side as well as the right side.

Compare the two ways of working the mosaic pattern. Notice that the pattern on the garter-stitch fabric looks a little broader and shorter, is nubby instead of smooth, and lies flat without curling at the edges. The photographs in this book usually show the patterns in the garter-stitch style, but any pattern can be worked either way. Or, you can combine the two fabrics by knitting the wrong-side rows of one color and purling the wrong-side rows of the other color; so you can vary the texture of your mosaic knitting to suit your own taste.

In seamless circular knitting, a mosaic pattern uses each color for 2 rounds instead of 2 rows, and all slip-stitches are always slipped with yarn in back. To make a stockinette-stitch fabric in circular knitting, *knit* all rounds; never purl. To make a garter-stitch fabric in circular knitting, knit the first round and purl the second round of *each* color. When purling, always pass the yarn to the back or wrong side of the work before slipping the slip-stitches, because in mosaic knitting the yarn *never* passes across the right side of a slip-stitch.

Seamless circular knitting is one of only two cases in which you have to pay attention to pattern multiples. Now that you know how to do mosaic knitting, you can see why a mosaic pattern can be worked on *any* number of stitches on a flat (not circular) piece; it is because a right-side row may end at any point in the pattern, and the next wrong-side row can pick it up at that point just as well as if you carried the last pattern repeat all the way to the left-hand edge of the chart. (Remember, though, when working a partial repeat at the end of a right-side row, always *knit* the final stitch of that row even if the chart calls for a slip-stitch in that position, to carry the yarn over to the left-hand edge.) However, in circular knitting, it's necessary to cast on an exact multiple of stitches for the pattern, *without* edge stitches, if you want the design to come out even at the end of each round. In this case you begin each round with the first stitch inside the chart's right-hand repeat line, and finish the round with the last stitch inside the chart's left-hand repeat line, never passing these repeat lines at all.

The other case in which you have to pay attention to pattern multiples is when you are using a pattern with an obvious central stitch, and want to place this stitch in the middle of a flat piece of knitting so the design will by symmetrical at both edges. Charts are a great help in planning this, because a chart clearly shows you the middle of the pattern and allows you to count the extra stitches in from each side edge. So a mosaic pattern need not begin at the right-hand edge of the chart, any more than it needs to finish at the left-hand edge. You can even draw an extra, temporary vertical line on the chart to show where such centered rows must begin to suit the number of stitches that you have. Remember, though, that the first right-hand edge stitch on every right-side row, like the last left-hand edge stitch, must be knitted, not slipped.

Think about these matters as you go on to work more mosaic patterns. If you feel that you have not fully understood the above information, reread it later after you have done more mosaic knitting. At the moment, though, you're going to do a final trial run on the same example pattern, which will show you still another aspect of the versatile mosaic technique.

Take your needles and yarn again, and cast on 35 stitches with the *dark* yarn. Knit 1 row. Join the light yarn and work from the example pattern chart (either stockinette-stitch fabric or garter-stitch fabric) *with colors reversed.* That is, use the black squares to represent your light yarn, and the white squares to represent your dark yarn. The result is a negative impression of the design as it appears on the chart. Sometimes a pattern treated in this way can look like an entirely different pattern, because reversing the dark and light colors may bring out different shapes that you saw previously as background spaces around contrasting motifs. This positive-negative treatment opens up many new possibilities. For instance, how about matched sweaters for a pair of twins, or his-and-hers or mother-daughter garments, worked in the same pattern with colors reversed? Later in this book, you'll encounter special shadow mosaic patterns that put the color-reversal idea to exciting use. So remember that in mosaic knitting, at least—if nowhere else—you may see black as white and white as black.

Now that you've worked the example pattern in both stockinette-stitch and garter-stitch fabrics, and in both positive and negative versions, and have learned to use a mosaic chart, you're ready to master all the other patterns in this book. If you're a beginner, you can practice by making some of the straight-strip projects and sampler-square designs described in chapter four. Later you can learn to shape mosaic-patterned fabrics into garments and other articles just as you shape any other type of hand-knit fabric. Shaping is easy when you work from a chart, because the pattern is always plainly visible on the chart in a direct visual correspondence with the knitting itself. Each single decrease, for example, knocks one square off the charted side edge so you can always see where each shortened row must begin in order to keep the pattern correct.

Anything you can make with knitting, you can make with mosaic patterns. The original designs in this book will give you many ideas for combining your own favorite colors with intriguing new pattern motifs to make your own creative projects.

General Information About Patterns

How do you see a black and white checkerboard? As black squares on a white background, or as white squares on a black background? Your immediate perception of any pattern in contrasting colors depends to some extent on your own visual preference for one of the colors. But with a small readjustment in your mental attitude, you can see that checkerboard first one way, then the other way. Mosaic patterns are like that. As you study each pattern, you should make the same kind of mental readjustment. Observe the design formed by the dark stitches, then look again and observe the design formed by the light stitches. Imagine how these two designs would appear with their colors reversed; or better yet, knit the pattern that way and see.

In some mosaic patterns (such as Bands 30, 35, 52, 53, and 55), the dark stitches carry a primary motif while the light stitches serve as a background. In others (such as Mosaics 13, 14, 39, 41, 42, 47, and all the shadow patterns), both colors display the same design while dark and light shapes interlock with each other, either vertically or horizontally, upside down or right side up. In the majority of mosaics, dark and light motifs are different but each one forms a coherent design of its own. A felicitous example of this type is Band 57, "Arbor Gate." Dark stitches form an arched gateway with double gates standing ajar; light stitches form a tree between the gates. Quite a few patterns arrange dark and light lines to resemble knots, plaits, chain links, or interlaced strands.

Designs for mosaic knitting tend to show a rectilinear geometry, due to the fundamental nature of the technique. Unlike cable knitting, which usually forms curves, or lace knitting, which usually forms diagonal lines, the mosaic fabric is constructed of double rows that run straight across and slip-stitches that run straight up. Therefore diagonal lines are suggested by stair steps, and most patterns are based on simple vertical-horizontal motifs such as the square, the cross, the right angle, the fret or Greek key design, and the fylfot, gammadion, or swastika. Parenthetically, concerning the swastika it should be noted (for those who know little of its long history except for its unsavory incarnation as a symbol of violence during the 1930's and '40's) that this device is as old as civilization, and in most of its previous incarnations it has represented a creative force—the sun, the universe, symbolic rebirth, long life, or good luck. It has been found on some of the oldest artifacts known, from Inca textiles to relics of Babylon and Troy. Around the dawn of history, various peoples evidently regarded the swastika as a sign potent with life-giving magic. But aside from that, it's a motif that lends itself to endless development in all sorts of rectilinear designs, and so you will see it (sometimes only after careful searching) embedded in a number of mosaic patterns.

A pattern is, by definition, symmetrical. Many mosaic patterns have bilateral symmetry; that is, the design is balanced and matched (in reverse) on each side of the center. Such patterns are best shown in balance on the knitted piece, with the center stitch of one motif right in the middle of the knitting. Nearly always, the center stitch will be found on the chart exactly midway between the side edges. If you are working on a number of stitches that will *not* accommodate an even multiple for your pattern, you can center it by dividing the odd leftover stitches and placing half of them at one side edge, half at the other. Then you will begin each row at some arbitrary point on the chart other than the right-hand edge, and end it at the corresponding point the same number of squares to the other side of the center.

Patterns that are off-center, or lacking bilateral symmetry, can start and stop anywhere. You don't have to bother centering them. But check your pattern chart carefully; there may be a center in the design that is not obvious at first. There may also be a surprise or two, in the form of subordinate motifs that are split by the edges of the chart and therefore don't show themselves whole until you knit more than one repeat. This is always true of half-drop patterns, in which the basic motif is staggered so that a second row of identical or reversed shapes are arranged in the spaces between those of the first row. Half-drop patterns are so called because the upper half of one motif occupies the same knitted rows as the lower half of an adjacent one. Examples of this kind of pattern treatment are numerous (see Mosaics 12, 25, 26, 40, 43, 49, 53, and many others).

Most people, even people accustomed to thinking in aesthetic terms, don't really perceive patterns as well as they think they do. Only a short time after looking at even a fairly simple, obvious design, they retain almost no mental image of what they have seen, cannot describe it, are only vaguely aware of how the lines and shapes relate to each other, and could not make a copy of the pattern if their lives depended on it. The well-known inability of the average witness in court to remember accurately what he has seen applies also to the average person's comprehension of patterns. What happens during such "seeing" is that the untrained observer passively allows his eye to be drawn to one or two of the principal focal points in the design and to stay there. This untrained observer gains only a hazy peripheral impression of the pattern's real arrangement.

However, with practice anyone can become a trained observer of patterns. The trick is to keep the eye moving. Follow each line, noting its angle and direction and way of intersecting with other lines. Notice the relative positions of dark and light shapes, and the points at which they interlock. Search for the main rhythmic structure of the design, and see how subordinate structures are placed. Observe the arrangement of motifs: are they repeated in vertical or horizontal lines, in both, or alternately as in a half-drop? Do they show themselves upside down as well as right side up? Is the pattern top-to-bottom reversible (looking the same if you turn it around), or not? Are there secondary motifs in addition to the principal ones? How does this pattern differ from another that looks superficially similar, or represents a variation on the same thematic material? How does this pattern resemble the other?

Look at the single unit of design shown on each chart. With your eye, isolate these single units in the knitted illustration and notice how they are joined together. Pay particular attention to any split units at the edges or corners of the chart, noting how they resolve themselves on being worked in several repeats. Training yourself to be aware of the details of a pattern will help you to avoid mistakes in the knitting. Incidentally, it is also an excellent exercise for your general powers of perception. After a little awareness training on mosaic patterns, you may find yourself noticing all sorts of things that escaped your eye before.

A pattern, like a joke, has a "point" that you either see or don't see. But unlike the point of a joke, it doesn't have to be perceived immediately in order to make its impression. You may perceive the point of a design idea only after studying it for several minutes. But this delay only enhances the effect, for then you can say to yourself "Aha! There it is!" and feel good about it.

Of course the best possible way to comprehend any pattern is to pick up yarn and needles and actually *knit* it. As you go through the chart square by square, working several repeats instead of the single design unit that the chart shows, you automatically perceive the relationships of the various shapes and lines. Teach yourself many patterns by making an afghan or some other article out of sampler squares (see chapter four). You'll find the charts very easy to read after a little practice. Best of all, you'll be knitting unique, new patterns that no one (except your author, of course) ever has knitted before. So everything you create in mosaic knitting will be truly original—and *that* is an incomparable source of satisfaction to anyone who loves to knit.

*Figure 2. Above: Mosaic 2, "Herring-
bone"; below: Mosaic 3*

Figure 2

MOSAIC 2: "Herringbone"

Multiple of 8 sts plus 3

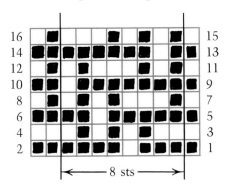

Figure 2

MOSAIC 3

Multiple of 8 sts plus 3

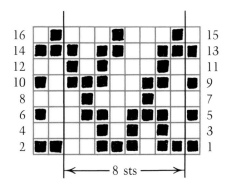

Figure 3

MOSAIC 4

Multiple of 8 sts plus 3

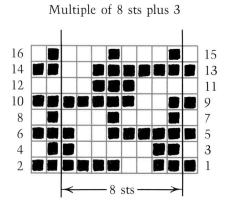

Figure 3

MOSAIC 5

Multiple of 8 sts plus 3

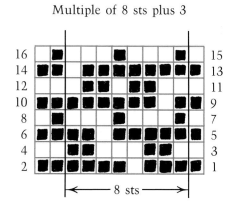

Figure 3. Above: Mosaic 4; below: Mosaic 5

Figure 4

MOSAIC 6

Multiple of 8 sts plus 3

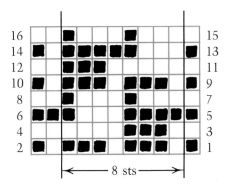

Figure 4

MOSAIC 7

Multiple of 8 sts plus 3

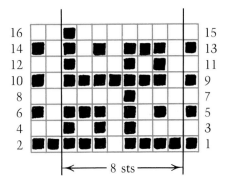

Figure 4. Above: Mosaic 6; below: Mosaic 7

Figure 5. Mosaic 8

Figure 6. Mosaic 9, "Crescents"

Figure 7. Mosaic 10, "Chain"

Figure 5

MOSAIC 8

Multiple of 8 sts plus 3

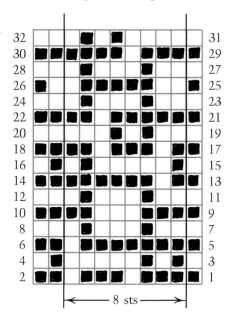

Figure 6

MOSAIC 9: "Crescents"

Multiple of 8 sts plus 3

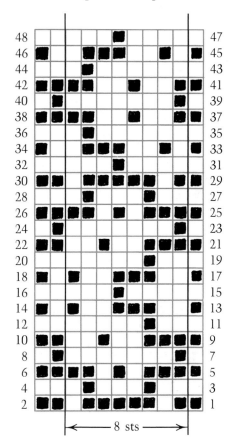

Figure 7

MOSAIC 10: "Chain"

Multiple of 10 sts plus 3

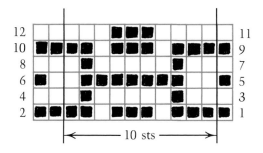

Figure 8. Mosaic 11

Figure 8

MOSAIC 11

Multiple of 10 sts plus 3

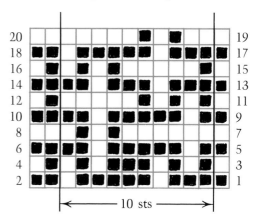

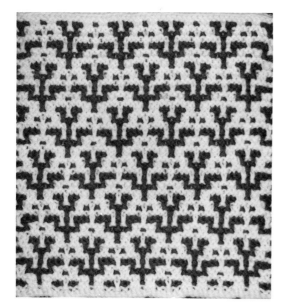

Figure 9. Mosaic 12, "Sprig"

Figure 9

MOSAIC 12: "Sprig"

Multiple of 10 sts plus 3

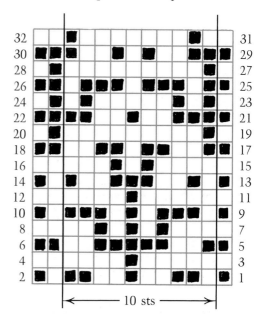

Figure 10

MOSAIC 13

Multiple of 10 sts plus 3

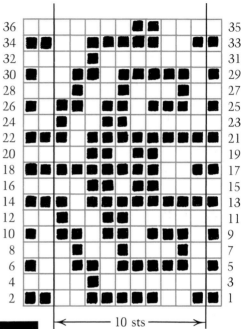

← 10 sts →

Figure 10. Mosaic 13

Figure 11. Mosaic 14

Figure 11

MOSAIC 14

Multiple of 11 sts plus 3

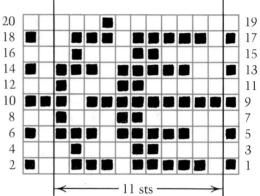

Figure 12. Mosaic 15

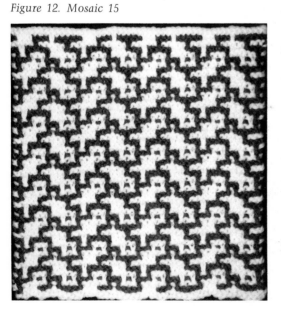

Figure 12

MOSAIC 15

Multiple of 12 sts plus 3

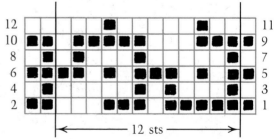

Figure 13

MOSAIC 16

Multiple of 12 sts plus 3

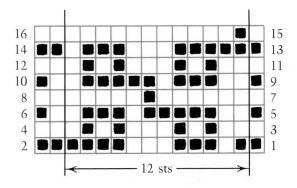

Figure 13. Mosaic 16

Figure 14

Figure 14. Mosaic 17

MOSAIC 17

Multiple of 12 sts plus 3

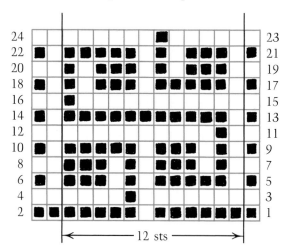

Figure 15

MOSAIC 18

Multiple of 12 sts plus 3

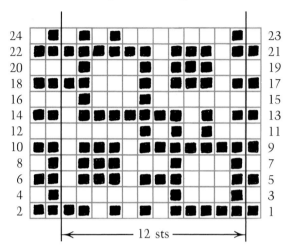

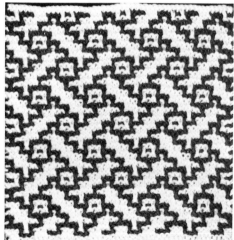

Figure 15. Mosaic 18

Figure 16

MOSAIC 19: "Basketweave"

Multiple of 12 sts plus 3

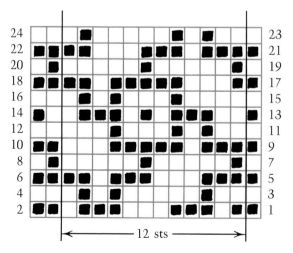

Figure 16. Mosaic 19, "Basketweave"

Figure 17. Mosaic 20, "Cable"

Figure 17

MOSAIC 20: "Cable"

Multiple of 12 sts plus 3

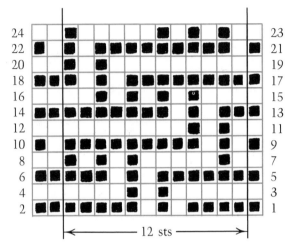

Figure 18. Mosaic 21

Figure 18

MOSAIC 21

Multiple of 12 sts plus 3

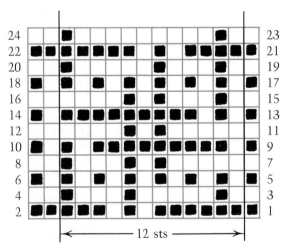

Figure 19

MOSAIC 22

Multiple of 12 sts plus 3

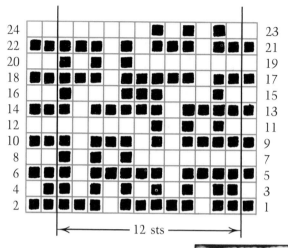

Figure 19. Mosaic 22

Figure 20

MOSAIC 23

Multiple of 12 sts plus 3

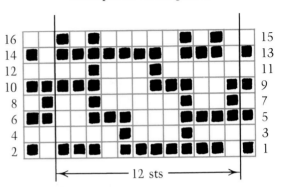

Figure 20. Above: Mosaic 23; below: Mosaic 24

Figure 20

MOSAIC 24

Multiple of 12 sts plus 3

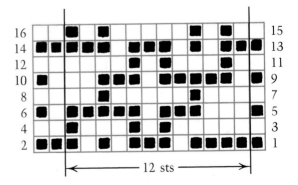

Figure 21

MOSAIC 25: "Crown"

Multiple of 12 sts plus 3

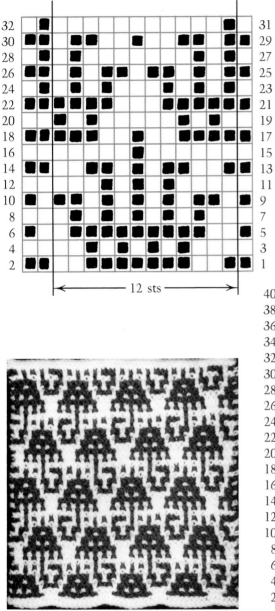

12 sts

Figure 21. Mosaic 25, "Crown"

Figure 22

MOSAIC 26: "Parasol"

Multiple of 12 sts plus 3

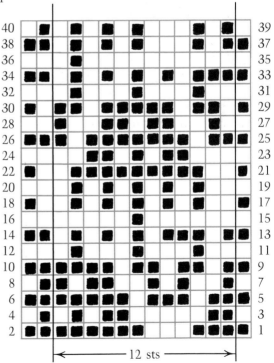

Figure 22. Mosaic 26, "Parasol"

12 sts

Figure 23

MOSAIC 27

Multiple of 10 sts plus 3

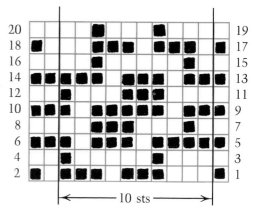

← 10 sts →

Figure 23

MOSAIC 28

Multiple of 10 sts plus 3

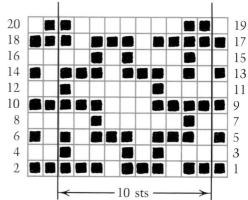

← 10 sts →

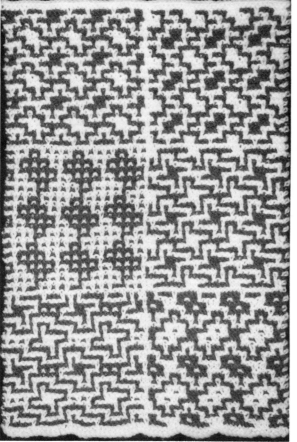

Figure 23. Variations on a Theme: Mosaics 27–32. Above, right: Mosaic 27; above, left: Mosaic 28; center, right: Mosaic 29; center, left: Mosaic 30; below, right: Mosaic 31; below, left: Mosaic 32

Figure 23

MOSAIC 29

Multiple of 10 sts plus 3

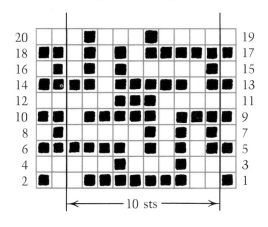

Figure 23

MOSAIC 30

Multiple of 10 sts plus 3

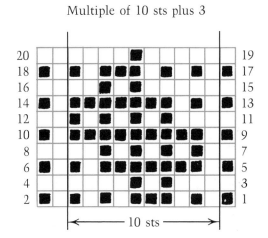

Figure 23

MOSAIC 31

Multiple of 10 sts plus 3

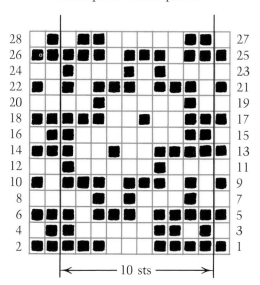

Figure 23

MOSAIC 32

Multiple of 14 sts plus 3

Figure 24. Sampler squares: Mosaics 33–36. Above, right: Mosaic 33; above, left: Mosaic 34; below, right: Mosaic 35; below, left: Mosaic 36

Figure 24

MOSAIC 33

Multiple of 14 sts plus 3

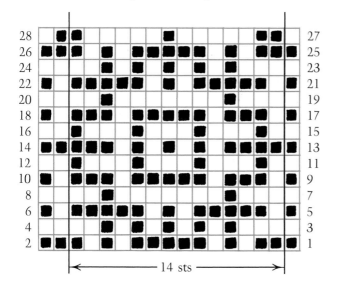

Figure 24

MOSAIC 34

Multiple of 14 sts plus 3

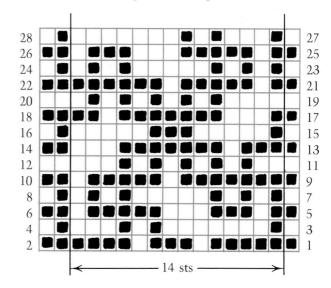

Figure 24

MOSAIC 35

Multiple of 14 sts plus 3

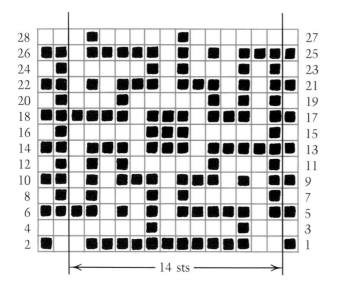

← 14 sts →

Figure 24

MOSAIC 36

Multiple of 14 sts plus 3

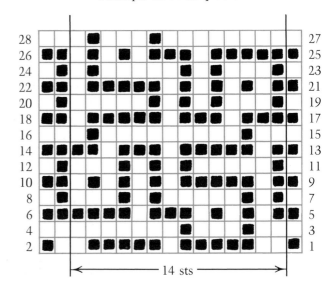

← 14 sts →

Figure 25

MOSAIC 37

Multiple of 14 sts plus 3

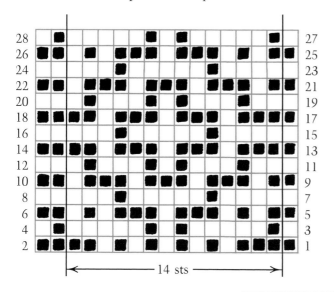

14 sts

Figure 25. Mosaic 37

Figure 26

MOSAIC 38

Multiple of 14 sts plus 3

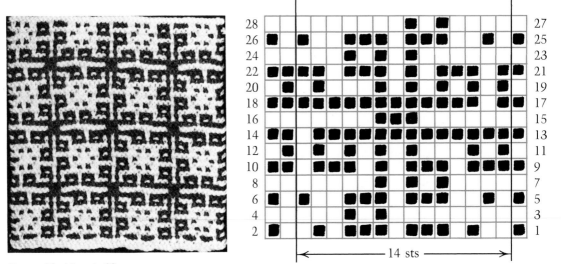

Figure 26. Mosaic 38

Figure 27

MOSAIC 39

Multiple of 14 sts plus 3

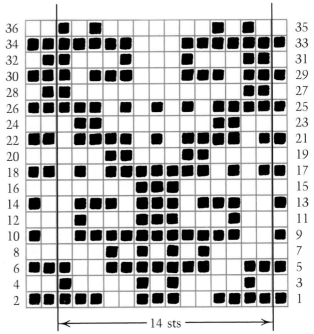

Figure 27. Mosaic 39

Figure 28

MOSAIC 40

Multiple of 14 sts plus 3

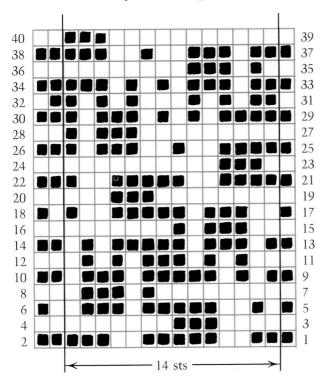

14 sts

Figure 28. Mosaic 40

Figure 29

MOSAIC 41

Multiple of 14 sts plus 3

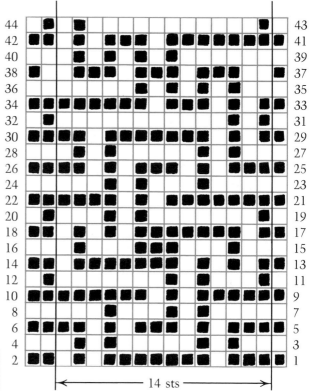

Figure 29. Mosaic 41

Figure 30

MOSAIC 42: "Ribbons"

Multiple of 14 sts plus 3

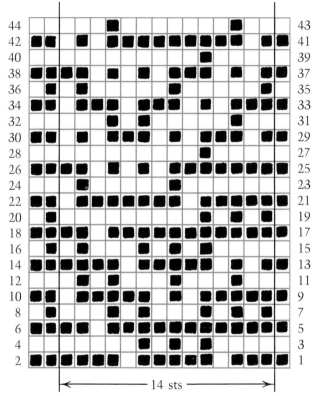

Figure 30. Mosaic 42, "Ribbons"

Figure 31. Mosaic 43, "Pseudoscorpion"

Figure 31

MOSAIC 43: "Pseudoscorpion"

Multiple of 14 sts plus 3

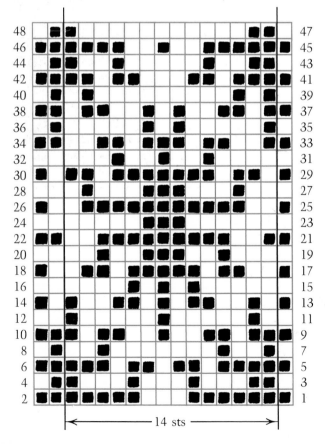

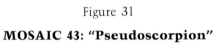

14 sts

Figure 32

MOSAIC 44

Multiple of 16 sts plus 3

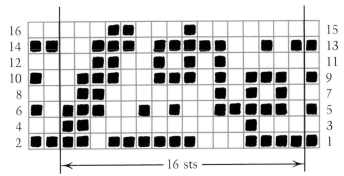

Figure 32. Mosaic 44

Figure 33

MOSAIC 45

Multiple of 16 sts plus 3

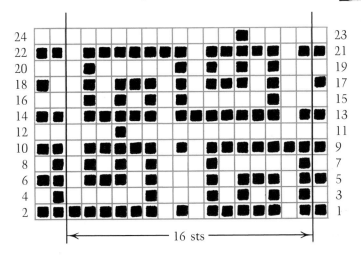

Figure 33. Mosaic 45

Figure 34

MOSAIC 46

Multiple of 16 sts plus 3

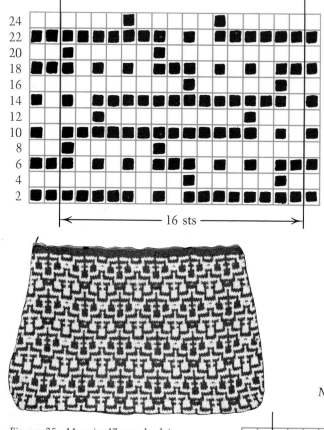

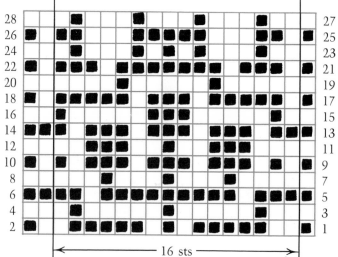

Figure 34. Mosaic 46

Figure 35. Mosaic 47, worked in a handbag

Figure 35

MOSAIC 47

Multiple of 16 sts plus 3

Figure 36

MOSAIC 48: "Garden Plot"

Multiple of 16 sts plus 3

Figure 36. Mosaic 48, "Garden Plot"

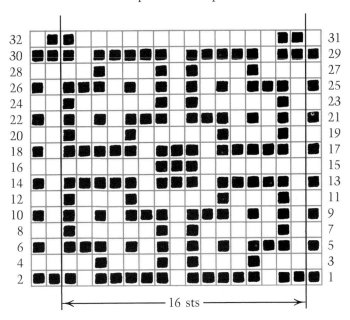

Figure 37

MOSAIC 49

Multiple of 16 sts plus 3

Figure 37. Mosaic 49

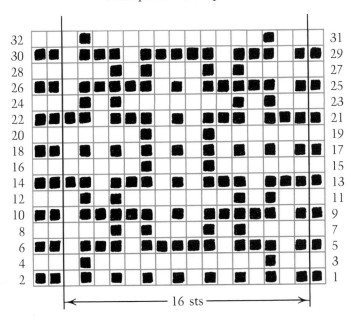

Figure 38. Mosaic 50

Figure 38

MOSAIC 50

Multiple of 16 sts plus 3

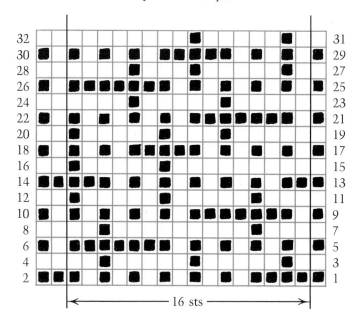

16 sts

Figure 39. Mosaic 51

Figure 39

MOSAIC 51

Multiple of 16 sts plus 3

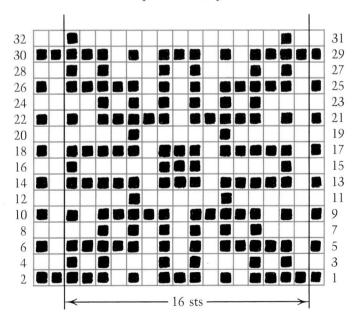

16 sts

Figure 40

MOSAIC 52

Multiple of 16 sts plus 3

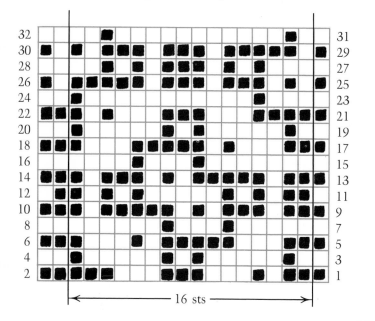

16 sts

Figure 41

MOSAIC 53

Multiple of 16 sts plus 3

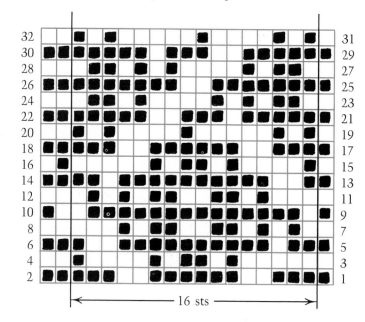

16 sts

Figure 40. Mosaic 52

Figure 41. Mosaic 53

Figure 42. Mosaic 54

Figure 42

MOSAIC 54

Multiple of 16 sts plus 3

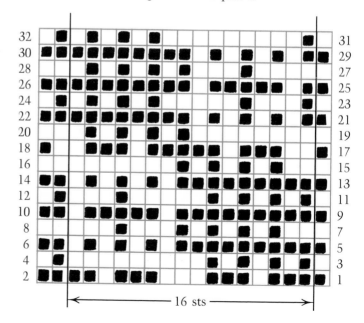

16 sts

Figure 43

MOSAIC 55

Multiple of 16 sts plus 3

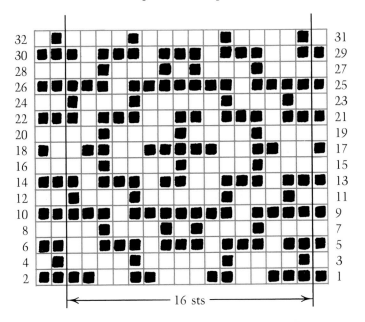

← 16 sts →

Figure 43. Mosaic 55

MOSAIC 56

Multiple of 16 sts plus 3

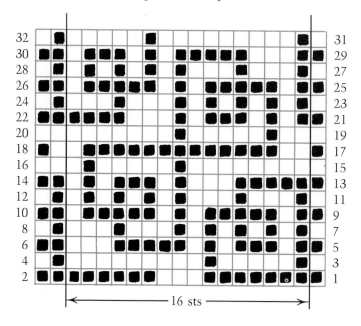

Figure 45

MOSAIC 57

Multiple of 16 sts plus 3

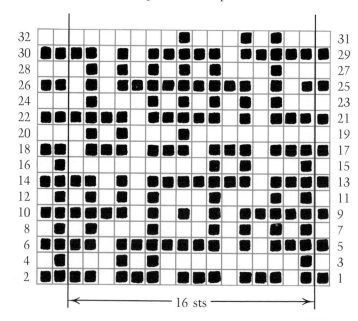

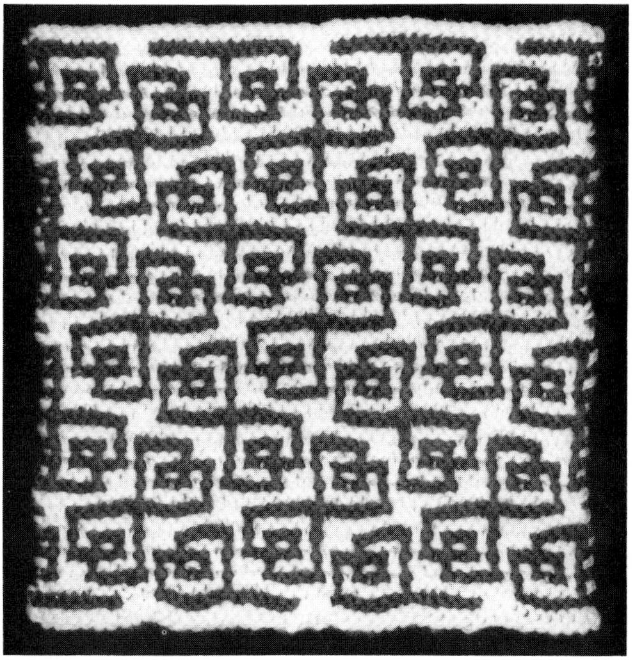

Figure 44. Mosaic 56

Figure 45. Mosaic 57

Figure 46

MOSAIC 58

Multiple of 16 sts plus 3

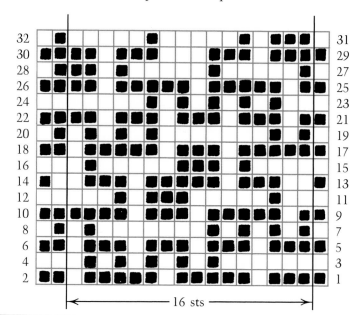

Figure 46. Mosaic 58

Figure 47

MOSAIC 59

Multiple of 16 sts plus 3

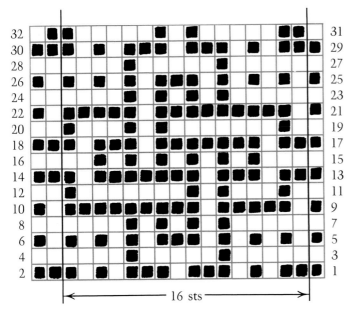

Figure 47. Mosaic 59

Figure 48

MOSAIC 60

Multiple of 16 sts plus 3

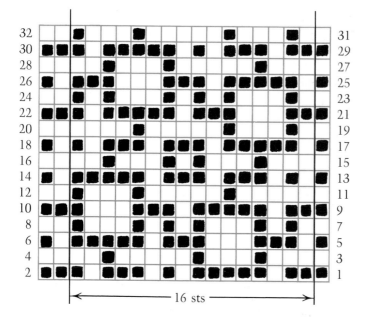

16 sts

Figure 48. Mosaic 60

Figure 49. Mosaic 61

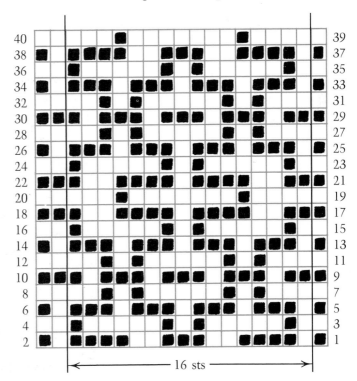

Figure 49

MOSAIC 61

Multiple of 16 sts plus 3

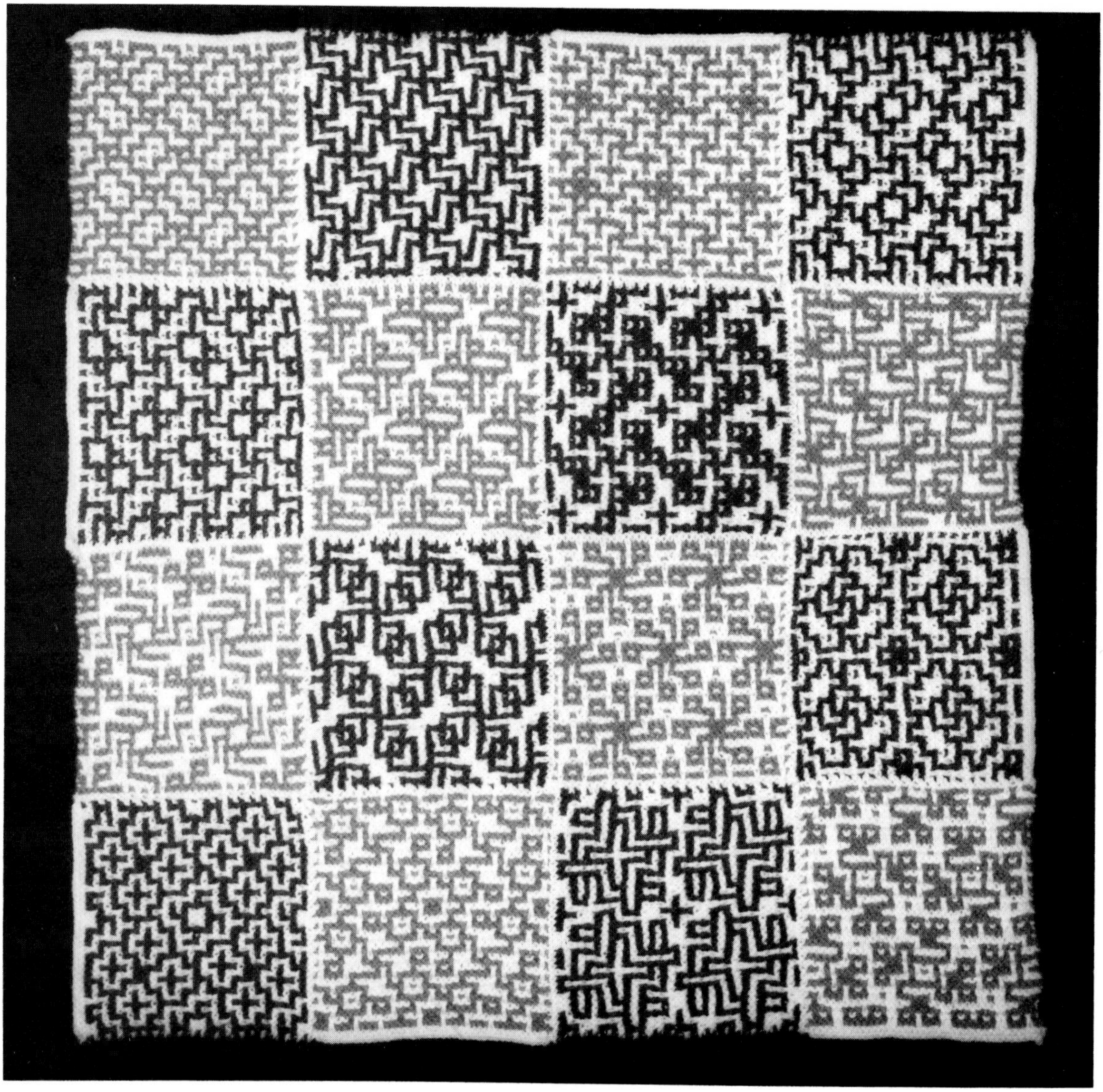

Figure 50. Sampler squares: sixteen variations on the Gammadion (swastika) Design, Mosaics 62–77. Above, left to right: Mosaics 62, 63, 64, and 65; second row, left to right: Mosaics 66, 67, 68, and 69; third row, left to right: Mosaics 70, 71, 72, and 73; below, left to right: Mosaics 74, 75, 76, and 77

Figure 50

MOSAIC 63

Multiple of 12 sts plus 3

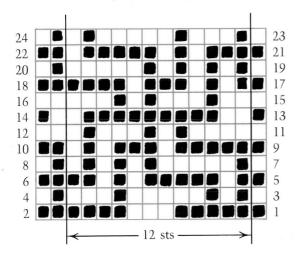

12 sts

Figure 50

MOSAIC 62

Multiple of 12 sts plus 3

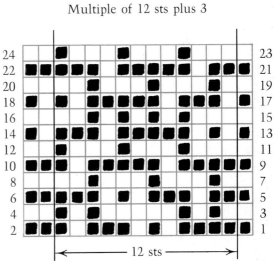

12 sts

Figure 50

MOSAIC 64

Multiple of 14 sts plus 3

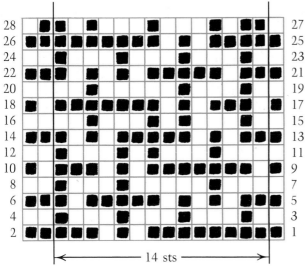

14 sts

Figure 50

MOSAIC 65

Multiple of 16 sts plus 3

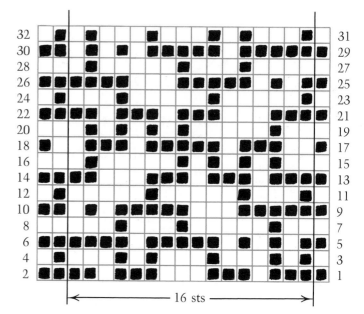

16 sts

Figure 50

MOSAIC 66

Multiple of 16 sts plus 3

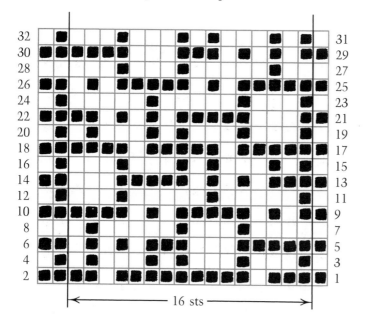

16 sts

Figure 50

MOSAIC 68

Multiple of 16 sts plus 3

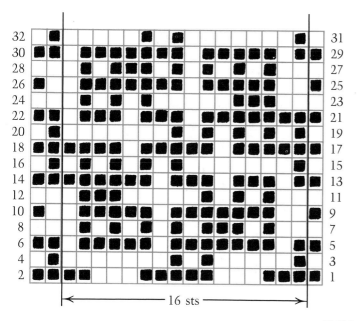

|← 16 sts →|

Figure 50

MOSAIC 67: "Windmill"

Multiple of 16 sts plus 3

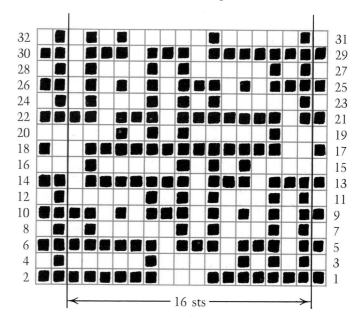

|← 16 sts →|

Figure 50

MOSAIC 69

Multiple of 16 sts plus 3

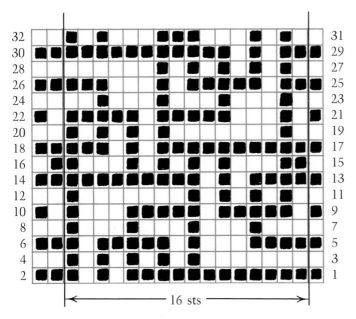

← 16 sts →

Figure 50

MOSAIC 70: "Twirl"

Multiple of 16 sts plus 3

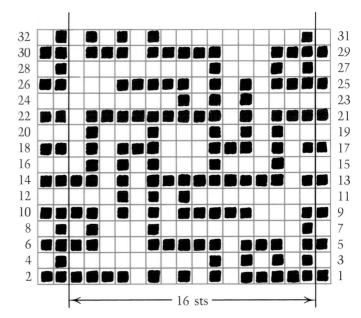

← 16 sts →

Figure 50

MOSAIC 71

Multiple of 16 sts plus 3

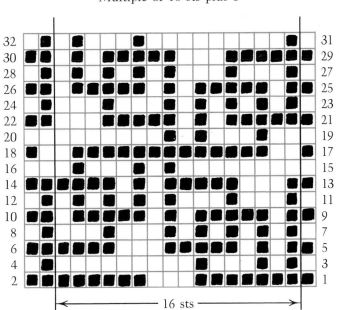

Figure 50

MOSAIC 72: "Pinwheel"

Multiple of 16 sts plus 3

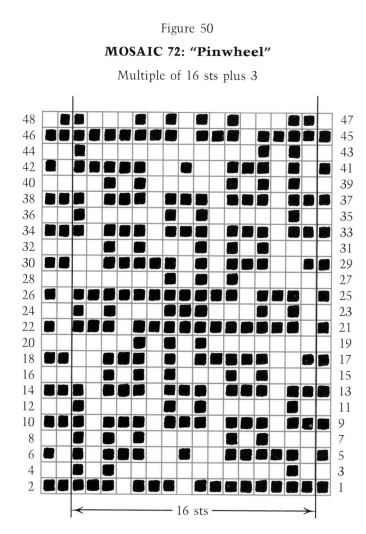

← 16 sts →

Figure 50

MOSAIC 73

Multiple of 18 sts plus 3

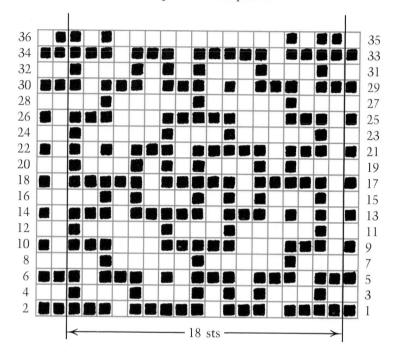

← 18 sts →

Figure 50

MOSAIC 74

Multiple of 18 sts plus 3

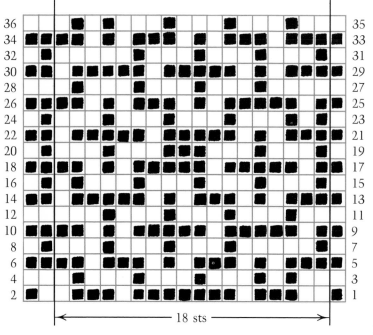

18 sts

Figure 50

MOSAIC 75

Multiple of 18 sts plus 3

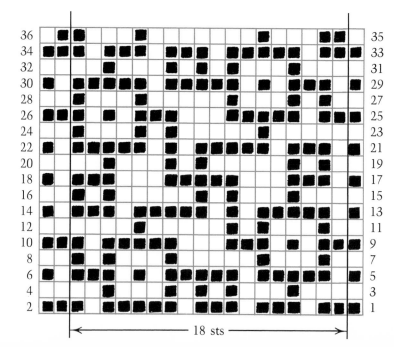

18 sts

Figure 50

MOSAIC 76

Multiple of 18 sts plus 3

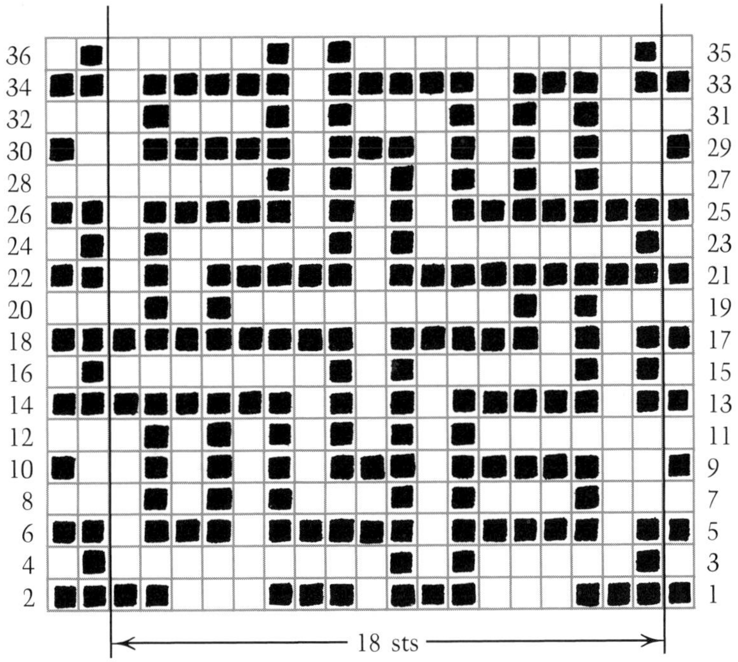

Figure 50

MOSAIC 77

Multiple of 18 sts plus 3

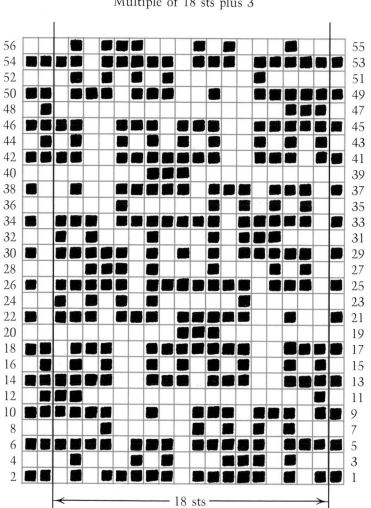

Figure 51

MOSAIC 78: "Branches"

Multiple of 18 sts plus 3

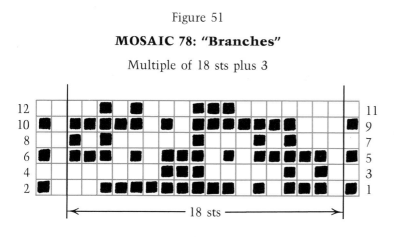

Figure 51. Mosaic 78, "Branches"

Figure 52. Mosaic 79

Figure 52

MOSAIC 79

Multiple of 18 sts plus 3

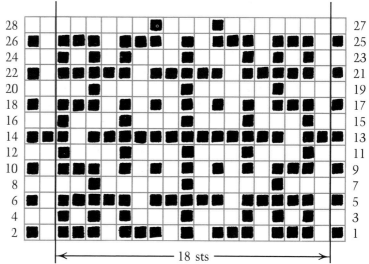

Figure 53

MOSAIC 80

Multiple of 18 sts plus 3

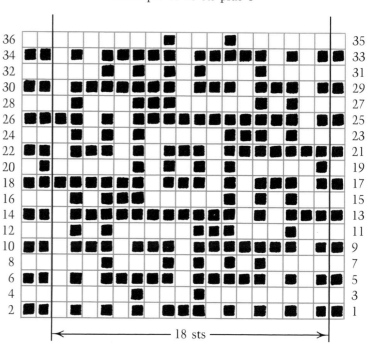

Figure 54

MOSAIC 81

Multiple of 20 sts plus 3

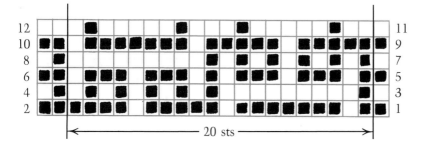

Figure 53. Mosaic 80

Figure 54. Mosaic 81

Figure 55. Mosaic 82

Figure 55

MOSAIC 82

Multiple of 20 sts plus 3

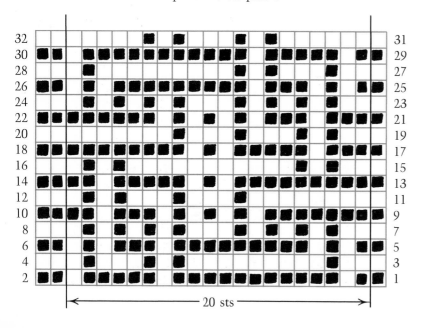

20 sts

Figure 56. Mosaic 83

Figure 56

MOSAIC 83

Multiple of 20 sts plus 3

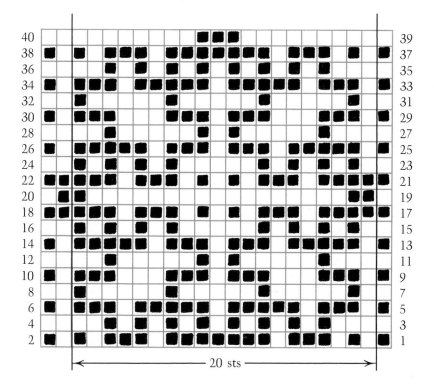

Figure 57

MOSAIC 84

Multiple of 20 sts plus 3

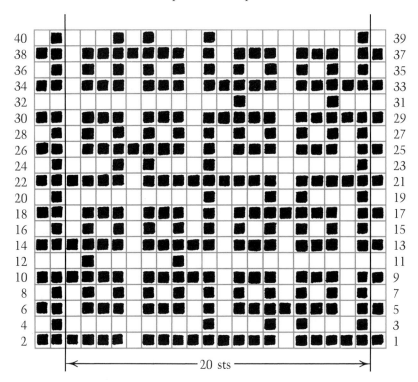

Figure 57. Mosaic 84

Figure 58

MOSAIC 85

Multiple of 20 sts plus 3

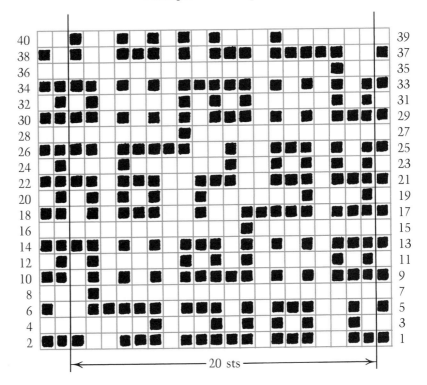

Figure 58. Mosaic 85

Figure 59

MOSAIC 86

Multiple of 20 sts plus 3

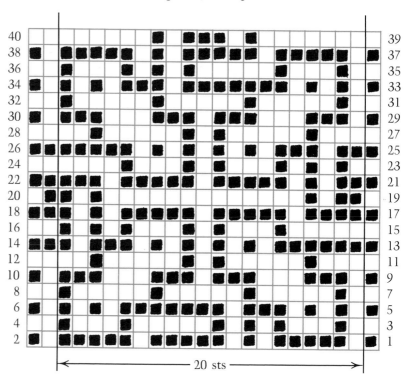

20 sts

Figure 59. Mosaic 86

Figure 60

MOSAIC 87

Multiple of 20 sts plus 3

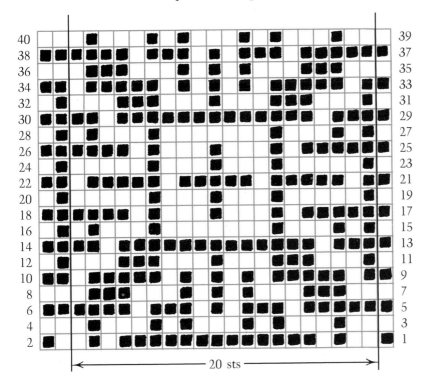

Figure 60. Mosaic 87

Figure 61

MOSAIC 88

Multiple of 20 sts plus 3

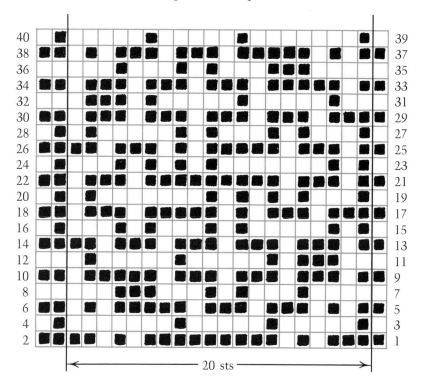

Figure 61. Sampler squares: Mosaics 88–91. Clockwise from upper left: Mosaics 88, 89, 90, and 91

Figure 61

MOSAIC 89

Multiple of 20 sts plus 3

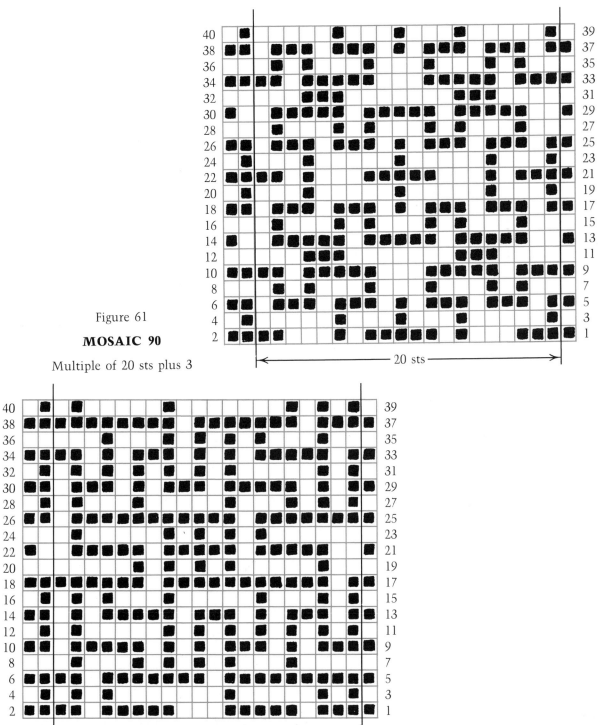

Figure 61

MOSAIC 90

Multiple of 20 sts plus 3

Figure 61

MOSAIC 91

Multiple of 20 sts plus 3

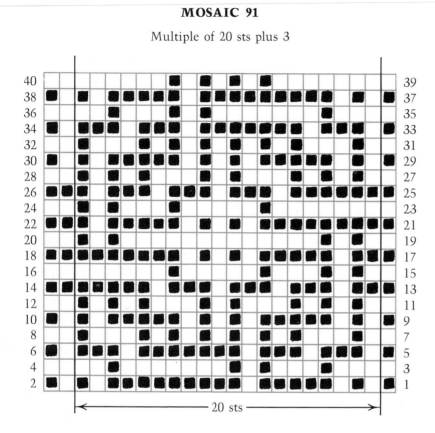

Figure 62. Sampler squares: Mosaics 92–95.
Clockwise from upper left: Mosaics 92, 93, 94,
95

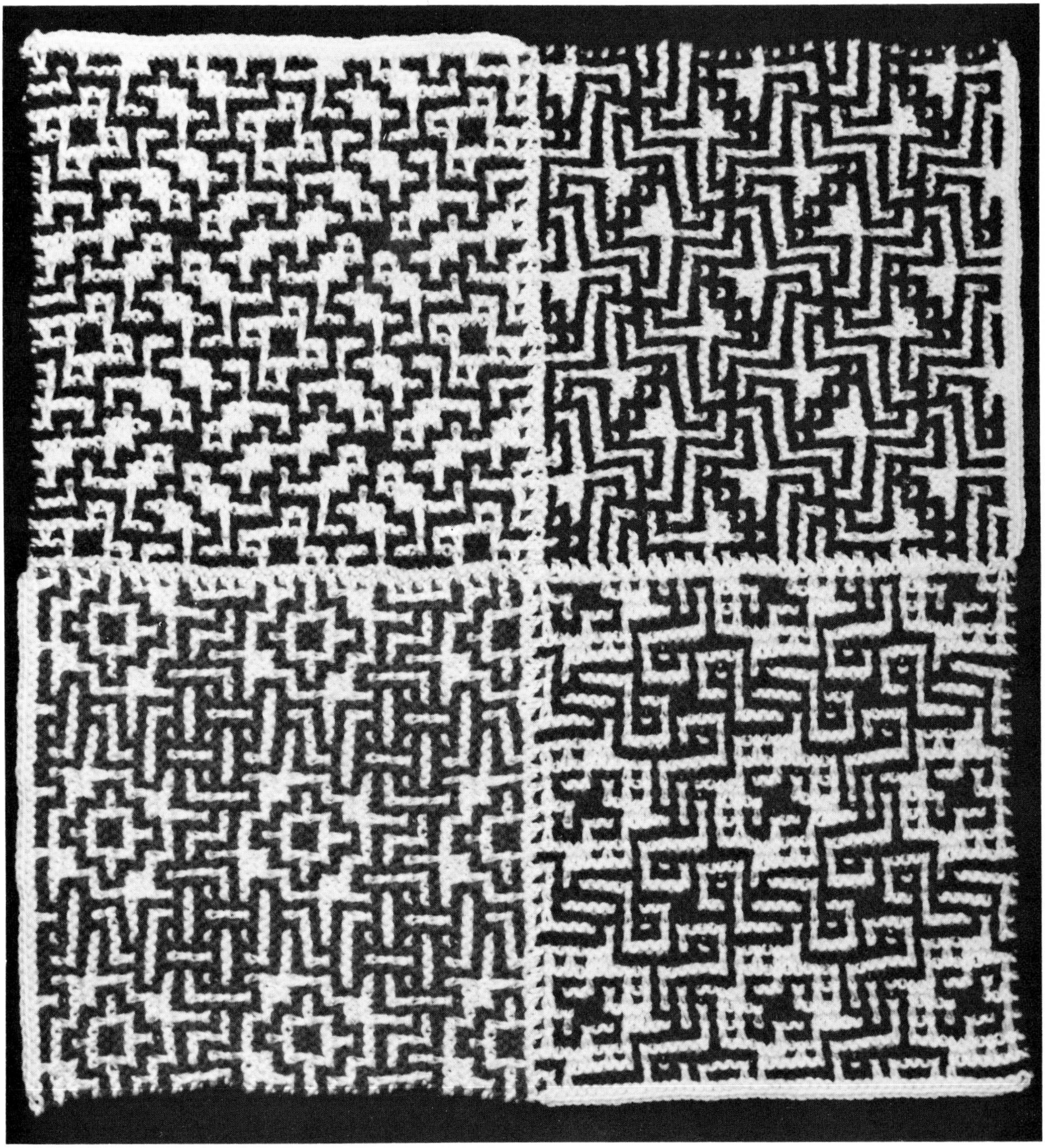

Figure 62

MOSAIC 92

Multiple of 20 sts plus 3

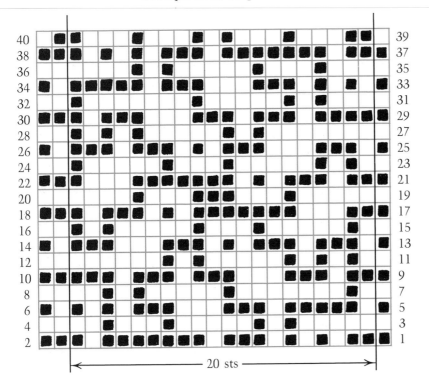

Figure 62

MOSAIC 93

Multiple of 20 sts plus 3

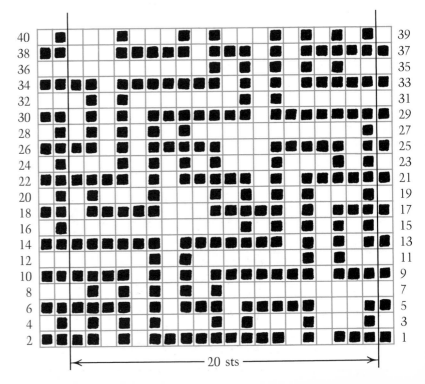

Figure 62

MOSAIC 94

Multiple of 20 sts plus 3

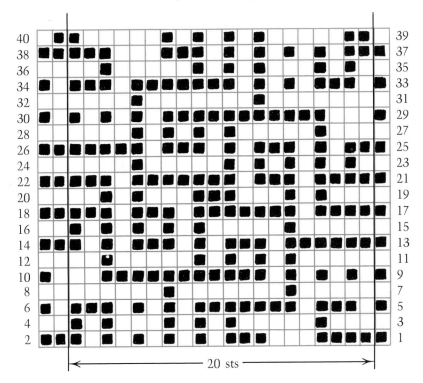

Figure 62

MOSAIC 95

Multiple of 20 sts plus 3

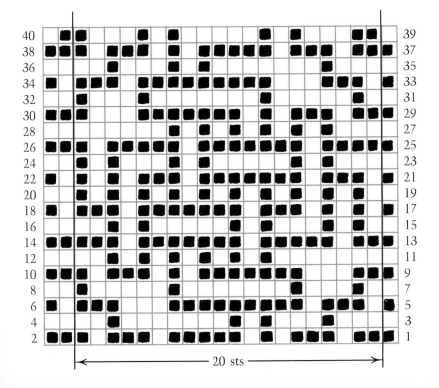

Figure 63. Sampler squares: Mosaics 96–99. Clockwise from upper left: Mosaics 96, 97, 98, and 99

Figure 63

MOSAIC 96

Multiple of 20 sts plus 3

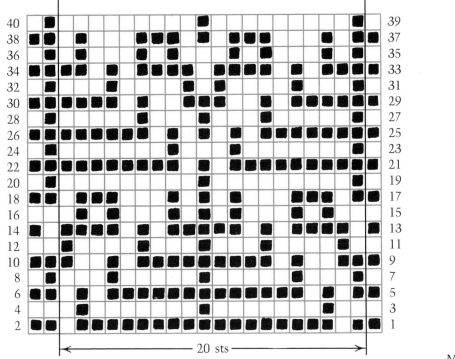

Figure 63

MOSAIC 97

Multiple of 20 sts plus 3

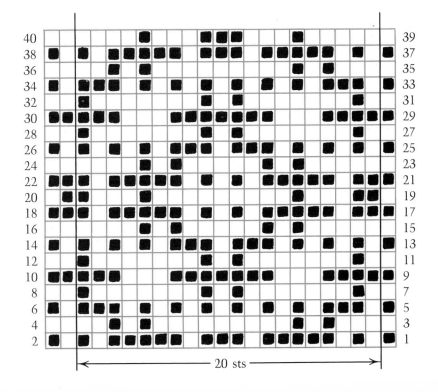

Figure 63

MOSAIC 98

Multiple of 20 sts plus 3

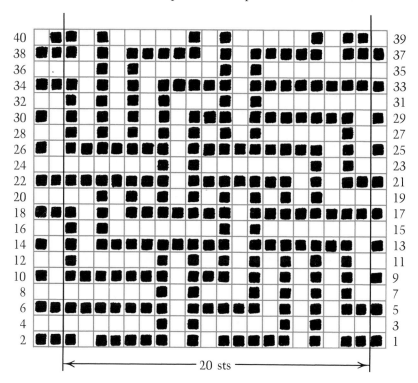

← 20 sts →

Figure 63

MOSAIC 99

Multiple of 20 sts plus 3

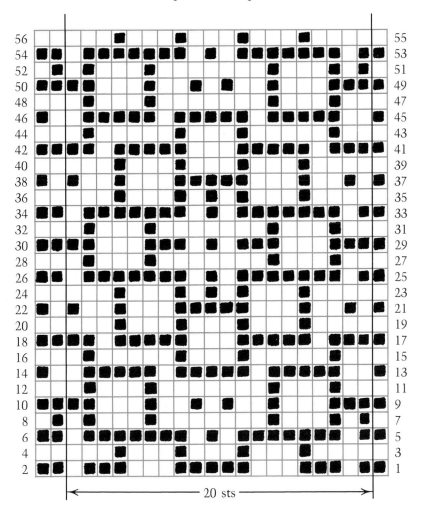

20 sts

Figure 64. Mosaic 100

Figure 64

MOSAIC 100

Multiple of 20 sts plus 3

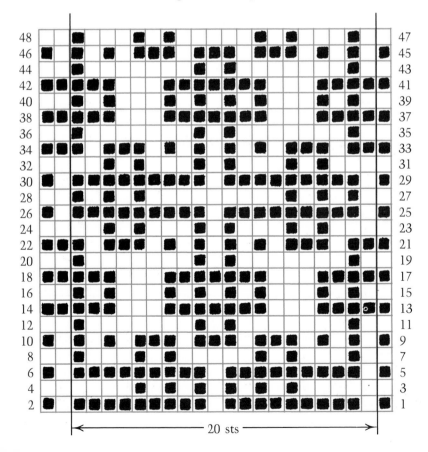

Figure 65. Mosaic 101

Figure 65

MOSAIC 101

Multiple of 22 sts plus 3

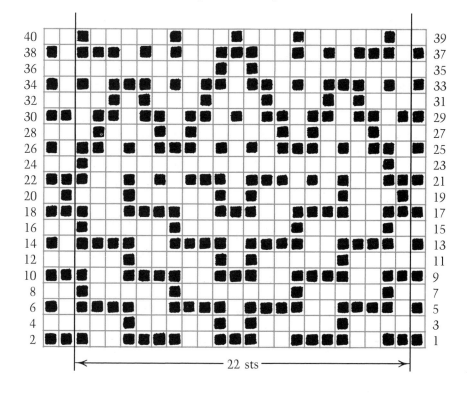

Figure 66

MOSAIC 102

Multiple of 22 sts plus 3

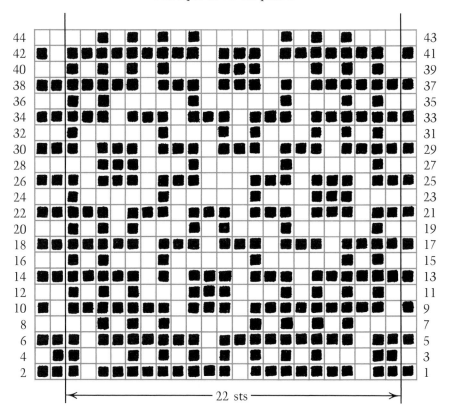

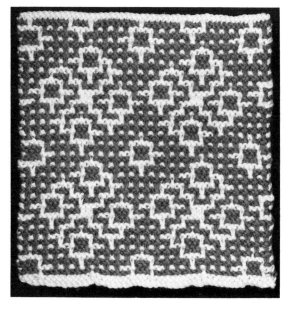

Figure 66. Mosaic 102

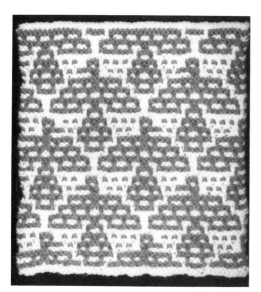

Figure 67. Mosaic 103, "Eagle"

Figure 67

MOSAIC 103: "Eagle"

Multiple of 22 sts plus 3

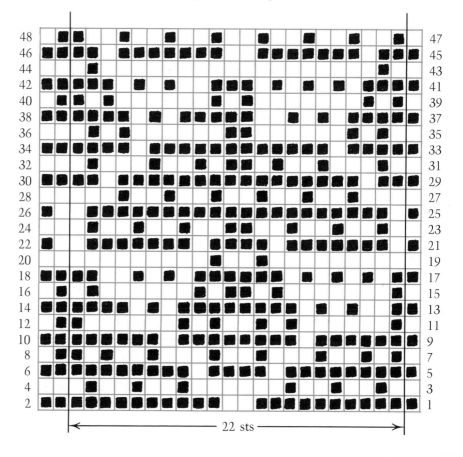

Figure 68

MOSAIC 104

Multiple of 24 sts plus 3

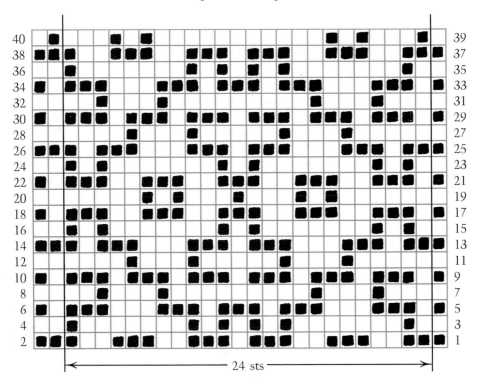

Figure 68. Mosaic 104

Figure 69

MOSAIC 105: "Puppy Dogs"

Multiple of 24 sts plus 3

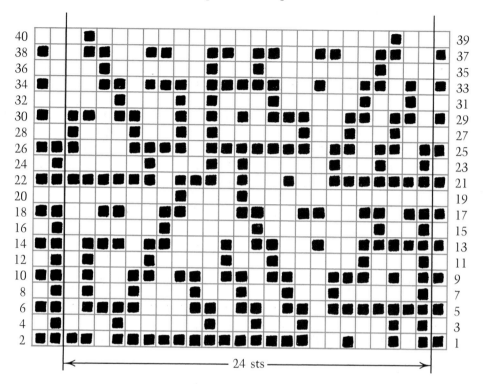

Figure 69. Mosaic 105, "Puppy Dogs"

Figure 70

MOSAIC 106

Multiple of 24 sts plus 3

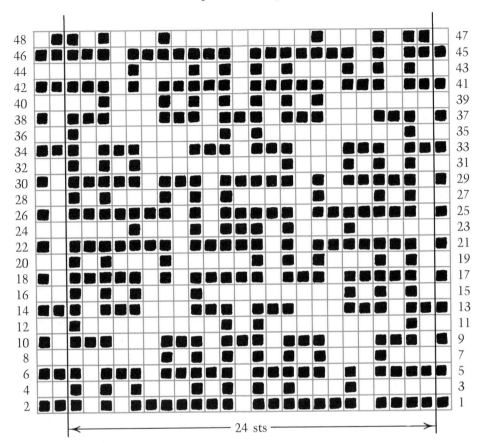

Figure 70. Mosaic 106

Figure 71. Mosaic 107

Figure 71

MOSAIC 107

Multiple of 24 sts plus 3

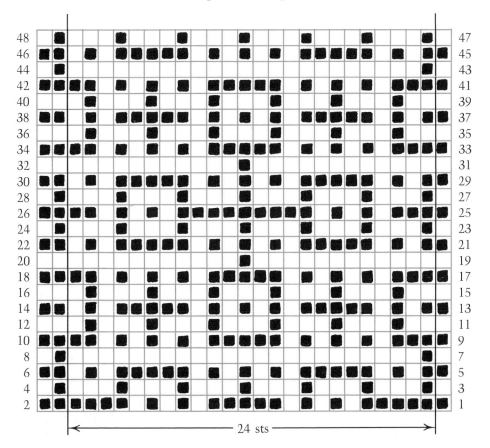

Figure 72. Mosaic 108, "Imps"

Figure 72

MOSAIC 108: "Imps"

Multiple of 26 sts plus 3

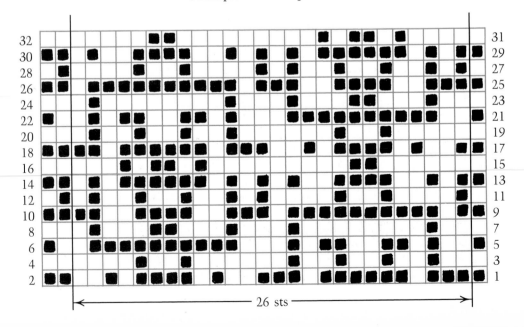

Figure 73

MOSAIC 109

Multiple of 32 sts plus 3

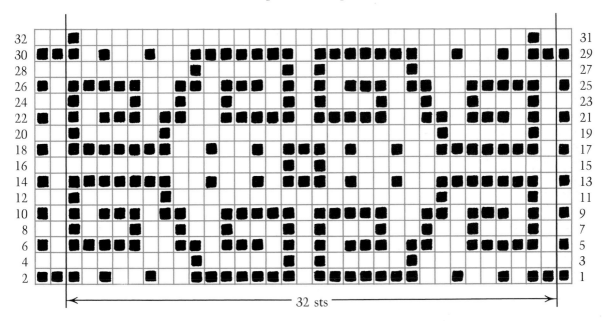

Figure 73. Mosaic 109

Figure 74

MOSAIC 110: "Cathedral"

Multiple of 32 sts plus 3

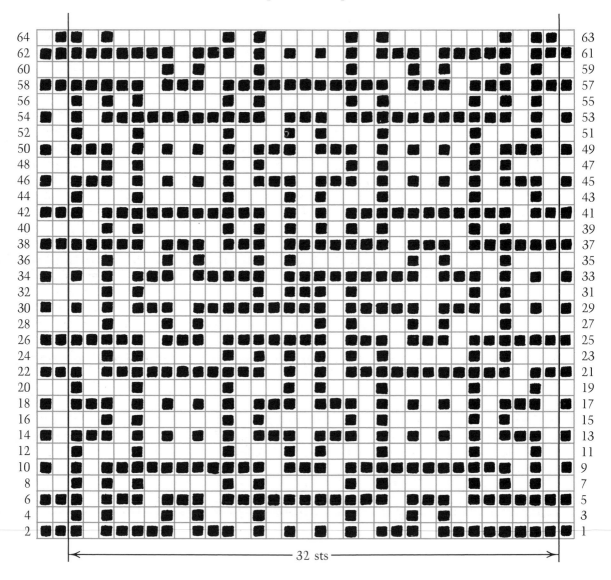

Figure 74. Mosaic 110, "Cathedral," worked in a table mat with a border of Band 81 (see next chapter)

2 / BAND PATTERNS

Any mosaic pattern that finishes with plain white rows across the top of its chart may be used as a decorative horizontal band when the pattern rows are worked just once through, or as a border design on picked-up stitches. Patterns of this kind are shown here in their own special section, even though they are not intrinsically different from other mosaic patterns. Any ordinary mosaic can be converted into a band pattern by ending it with a couple of plain rows at some point in the design. Conversely, any band pattern can be converted into an ordinary all-over mosaic by simple repetition of the same set of rows. Among the original designs in this book you'll see examples of both treatments. In this chapter, band patterns 1–13 are shown together in a straight strip for a poncho; band patterns 14–26 are shown together in a seamless banded skirt; band patterns 27–39 are shown as all-over designs created by repetition of their pattern rows; and the rest are shown in various combinations on their swatches. In the designs for garments and other articles described in chapter four, you'll find band patterns (plus mosaic and shadow patterns treated as bands) used in all sorts of ways.

Narrow bands having a small number of rows are useful for collars, cuffs, belts, hatbands, button bands, pocket and seam trims, hems, and edgings. Band patterns may be worked into the midst of a piece of knitting, or on picked-up stitches along an edge, or as separate strips for appliqué trim.

Remember that each band pattern, like all other patterns in this book, begins with plain white rows that are not shown on the chart. Therefore, to pick up stitches for a border (as along the side or neck edge of a garment), you'd attach the yarn represented by white squares and, with right side of the work facing you, pick up the first row of border stitches with this yarn. Turn the work and knit a wrong-side foundation row; or, if you're making a border in circular knitting, purl a foundation round. Then attach the yarn represented by black squares and begin Row 1 of your chosen pattern. Borders are best worked in a garter-stitch fabric so they will not curl. Finish your border with the two rows of white yarn shown at the top of the chart, then bind off firmly on the right side.

Figure 75. Bottom to top:
Bands 1, 2, 3, 4, 5, 6, 7, 8,
9, 10, 11, 12, and 13

Figure 75

BAND 1

Multiple of 8 sts plus 3

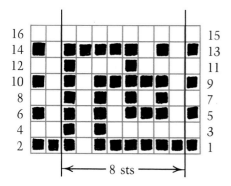

Figure 75

BAND 2

Multiple of 12 sts plus 3

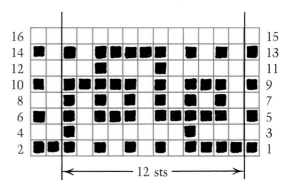

Figure 75

BAND 3

Multiple of 20 sts plus 3

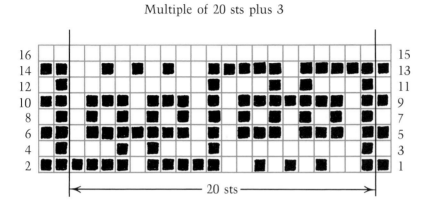

Figure 75

BAND 4

Multiple of 12 sts plus 3

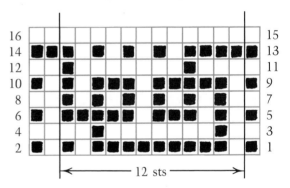

Figure 75

BAND 5

Multiple of 8 sts plus 3

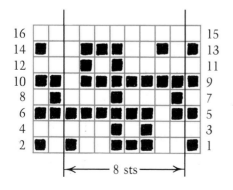

Figure 75

BAND 6

Multiple of 20 sts plus 3

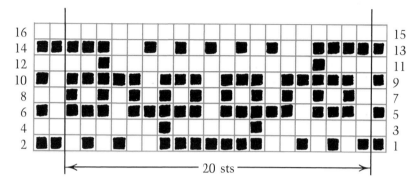

Figure 75

BAND 7

Multiple of 12 sts plus 3

Figure 75

BAND 8

Multiple of 16 sts plus 3

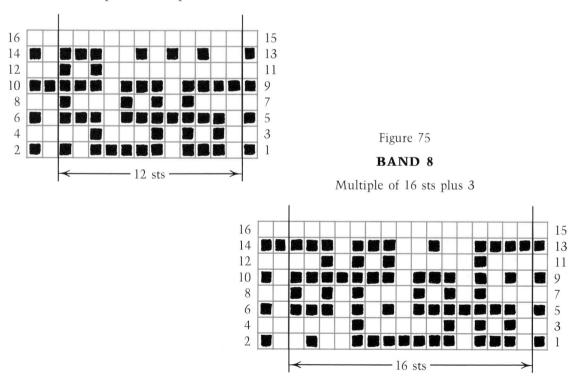

Figure 75

BAND 9

Multiple of 12 sts plus 3

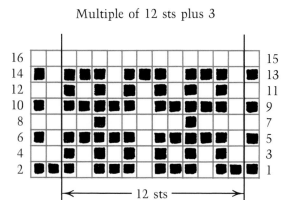

Figure 75

BAND 10

Multiple of 10 sts plus 3

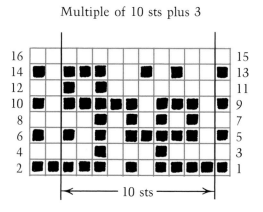

Figure 75

BAND 11

Multiple of 12 sts plus 3

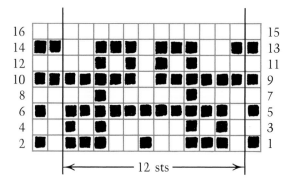

Figure 75

BAND 12

Multiple of 28 sts plus 3

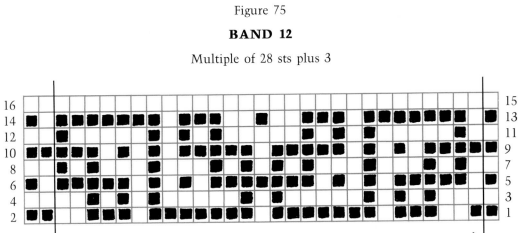

28 sts

Figure 75

BAND 13

Multiple of 12 sts plus 3

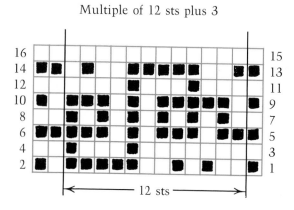

Figure 76

BAND 14

Multiple of 16 sts plus 3

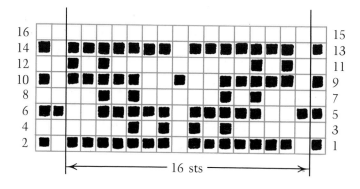

OPPOSITE: *Figure 76. Seamless skirt worked in (top to bottom) Bands 14, 15, 16, 17, 18, 19, 20, 21, 22, 23, 24, 25, and 26*

Figure 76

BAND 15

Multiple of 14 sts plus 3

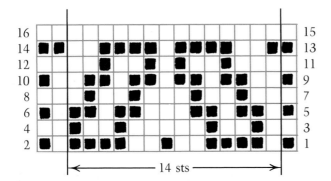

14 sts

Figure 76

BAND 16

Multiple of 8 sts plus 3

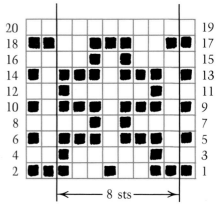

8 sts

Figure 76

BAND 17

Multiple of 20 sts plus 3

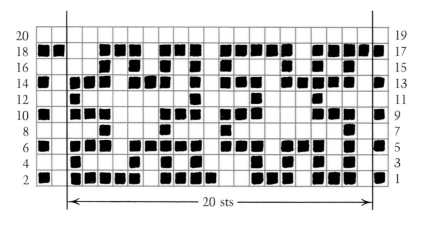

20 sts

Figure 76

BAND 18

Multiple of 12 sts plus 3

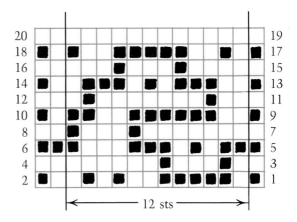

12 sts

Figure 76

BAND 19

Multiple of 24 sts plus 3

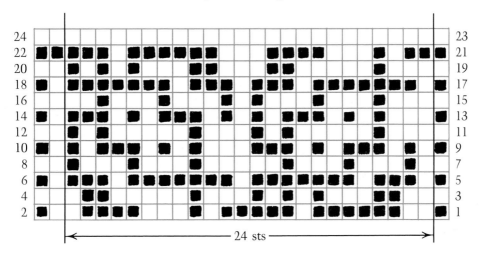

24 sts

Figure 76

BAND 20: "Large Chain"

Multiple of 12 sts plus 3

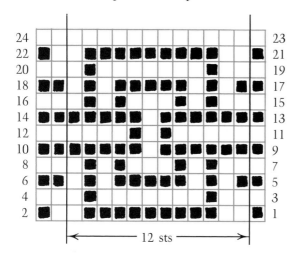

Figure 76

BAND 21

Multiple of 16 sts plus 3

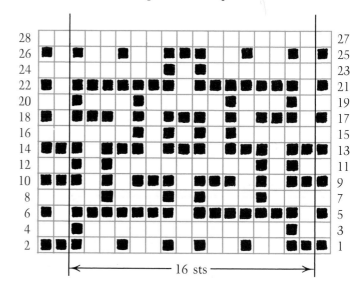

Figure 76

BAND 22

Multiple of 10 sts plus 3

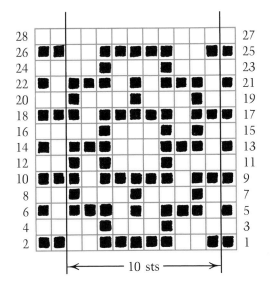

Figure 76

BAND 23: "Flying Bird"

Multiple of 12 sts plus 3

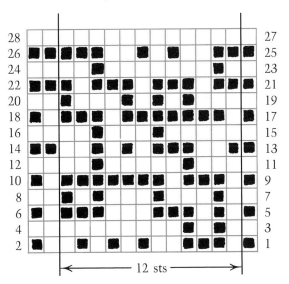

Figure 76

BAND 24

Multiple of 16 sts plus 3

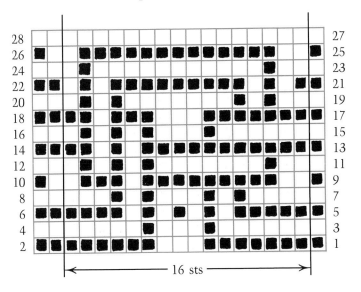

Figure 76

BAND 25

Multiple of 16 sts plus 3

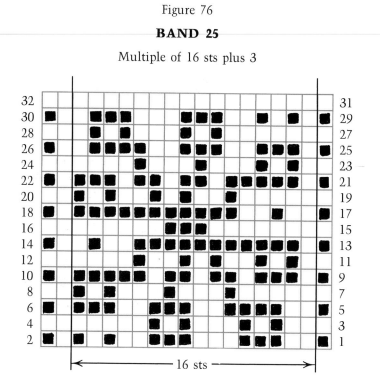

16 sts

Figure 76

BAND 26

Multiple of 16 sts plus 3

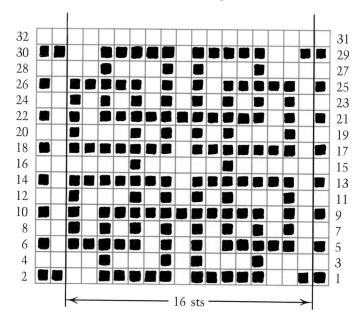

16 sts

Figure 77

BAND 27

Multiple of 10 sts plus 3

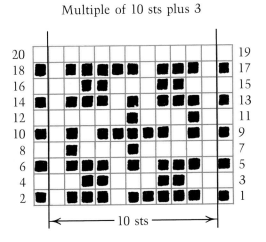

Figure 77. Band 27

Figure 78

BAND 28

Multiple of 12 sts plus 3

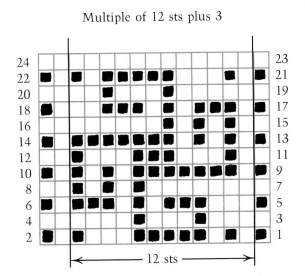

Figure 78. Band 28

Figure 79

BAND 29

Multiple of 12 sts plus 3

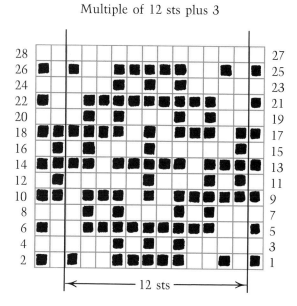

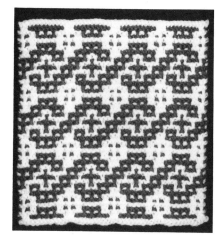

Figure 79. Band 29

Figure 80

BAND 30: "Watchdog"

Multiple of 13 sts plus 3

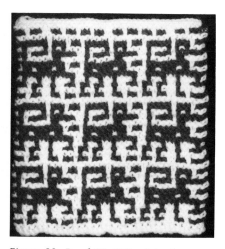

Figure 80. Band 30, "Watchdog"

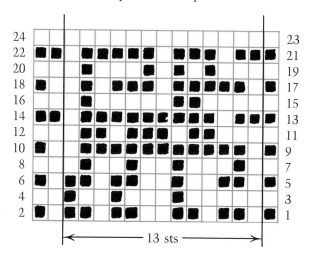

Figure 81

BAND 31: "Butterfly"

Multiple of 14 sts plus 3

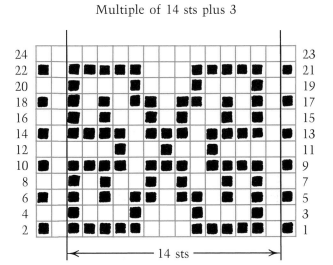

Figure 81. Band 31, "Butterfly"

Figure 82

BAND 32

Multiple of 16 sts plus 3

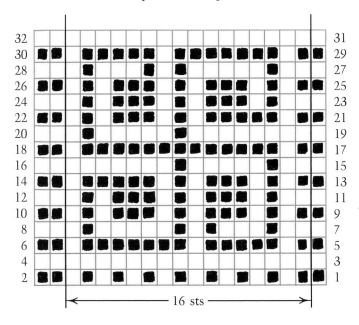

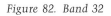

Figure 82. Band 32

Figure 83

BAND 33: "Diamond"

Multiple of 16 sts plus 3

Figure 83. Band 33, "Diamond"

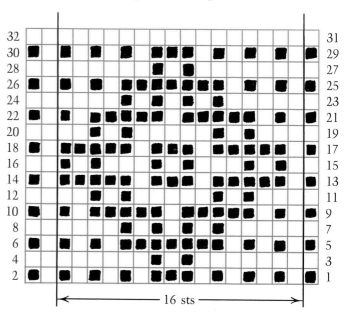

Figure 84

BAND 34

Multiple of 17 sts plus 3

Figure 84. Band 34

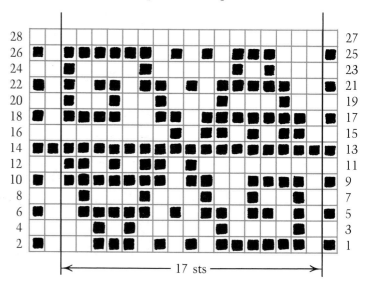

Figure 85

BAND 35: "Century Bird"

Multiple of 20 sts plus 3

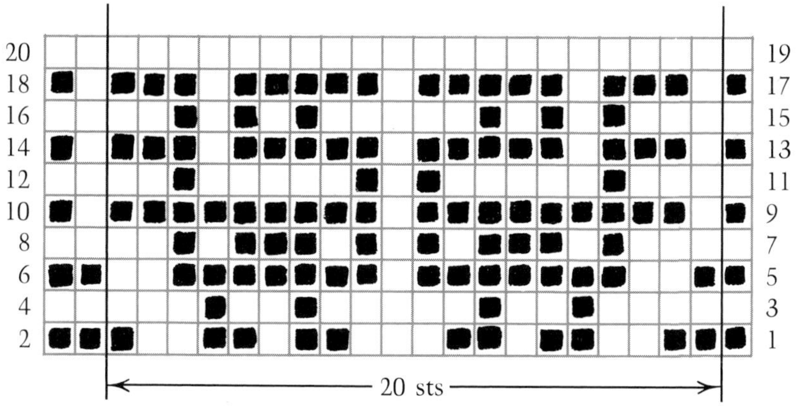

Figure 85. Band 35,
"Century Bird"

Figure 86

BAND 36

Multiple of 22 sts plus 3

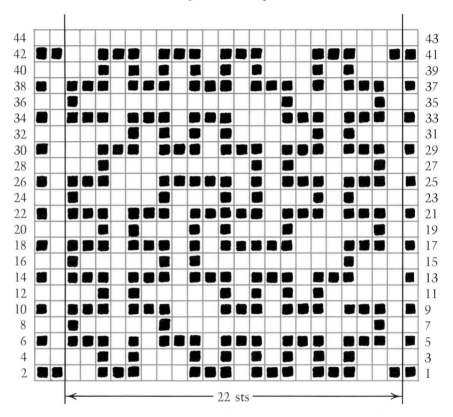

Figure 86. Band 36

Figure 87

BAND 37

Multiple of 24 sts plus 3

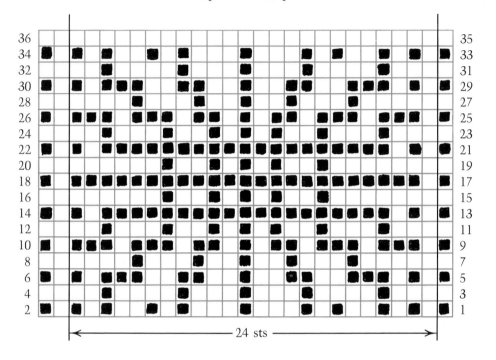

Figure 87. Band 37

Figure 88. Band 38

Figure 88

BAND 38

Multiple of 24 sts plus 3

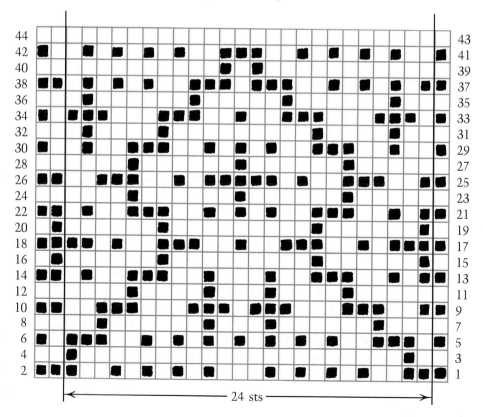

← 24 sts →

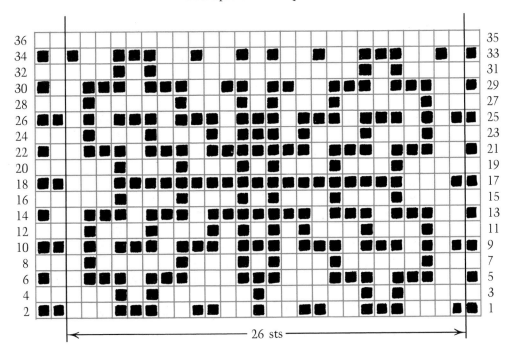

Figure 89. Band 39, "Large Butterfly"

Figure 89

BAND 39: "Large Butterfly"

Multiple of 26 sts plus 3

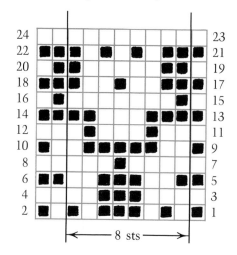

Figure 90

BAND 40

Multiple of 8 sts plus 3

8 sts

Figure 90

BAND 41

Multiple of 10 sts plus 3

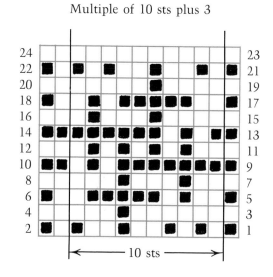

10 sts

Figure 90. Top to bottom: Bands 40, 41, 42, 43, 44, 45, 46, 47, 48, and 49

Figure 90

BAND 42

Multiple of 20 sts plus 3

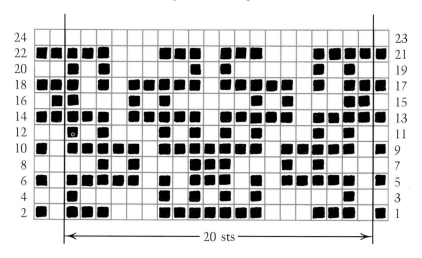

20 sts

Figure 90

BAND 43

Multiple of 10 sts plus 3

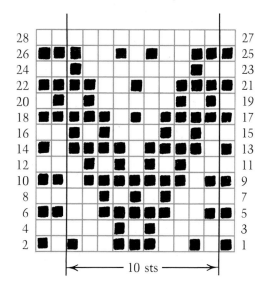

10 sts

Figure 90

120 / MOSAIC KNITTING

BAND 44

Multiple of 8 sts plus 3

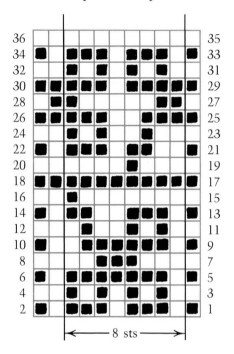

8 sts

Figure 90

BAND 45

Multiple of 14 sts plus 3

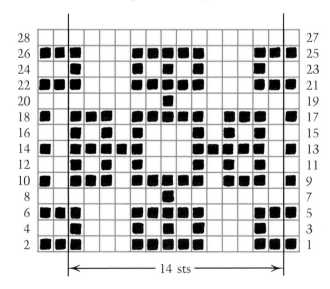

14 sts

Figure 90

BAND 46

Multiple of 18 sts plus 3

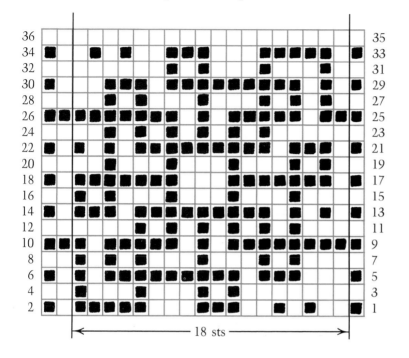

Figure 90

BAND 47

Multiple of 10 sts plus 3

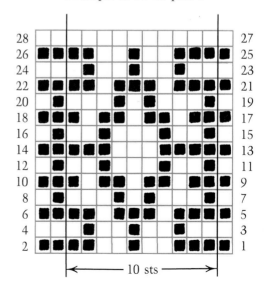

Figure 90

BAND 48

Multiple of 20 sts plus 3

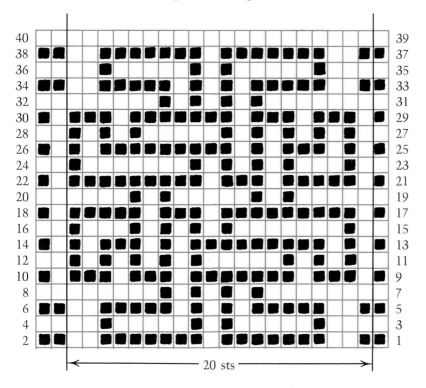

20 sts

Figure 90

BAND 49

Multiple of 16 sts plus 3

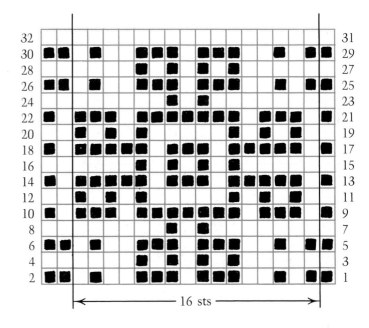

16 sts

Figure 91

BAND 50

Multiple of 8 sts plus 3

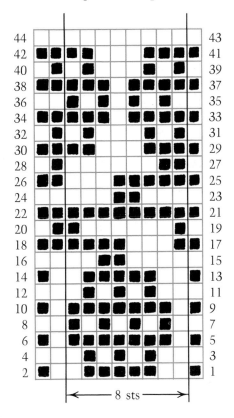

Figure 91. Top to bottom: Bands 50, 51, 52, 53, 54, 55, 56, and 57

Figure 91

BAND 51

Multiple of 10 sts plus 3

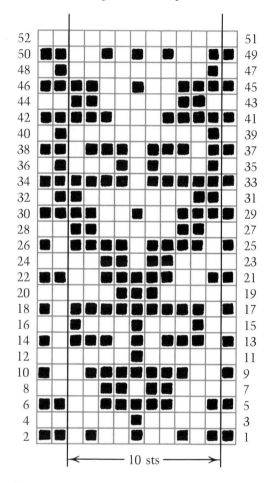

Figure 91

BAND 52: "Staghead"

Multiple of 16 sts plus 3

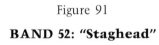

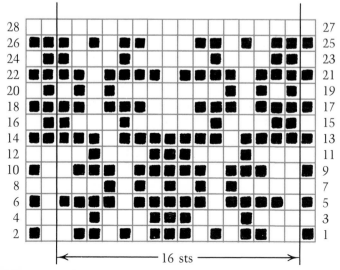

Figure 91

BAND 53: "Roses"

Multiple of 22 sts plus 3

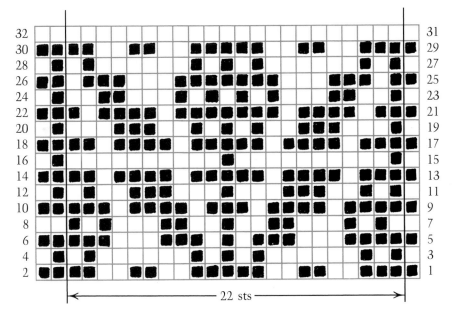

22 sts

Figure 91

BAND 54

Multiple of 28 sts plus 3

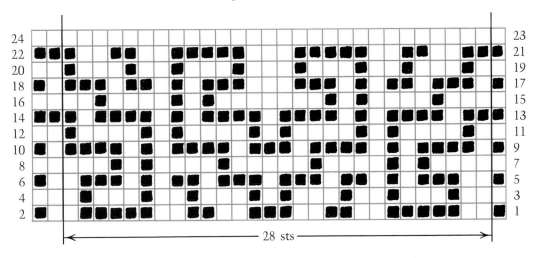

28 sts

Figure 91

BAND 55: "Acrobats"

Multiple of 16 sts plus 3

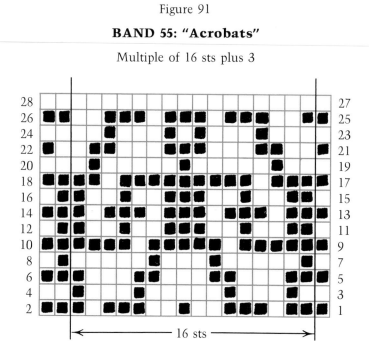

← 16 sts →

Figure 91

BAND 56

Multiple of 22 sts plus 3

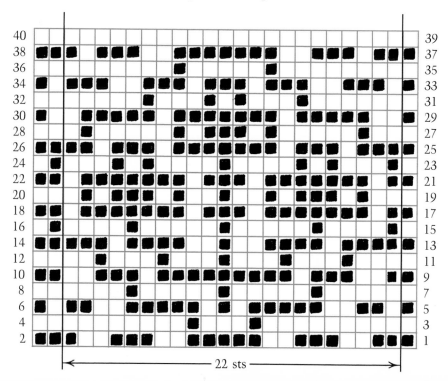

← 22 sts →

Figure 91

BAND 57: "Arbor Gate"

Multiple of 21 sts plus 3

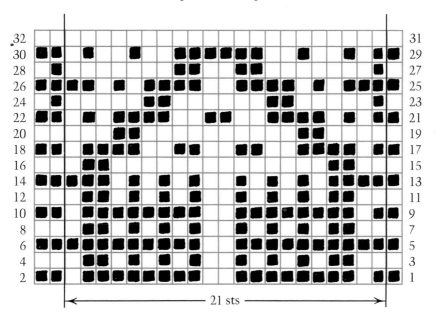

21 sts

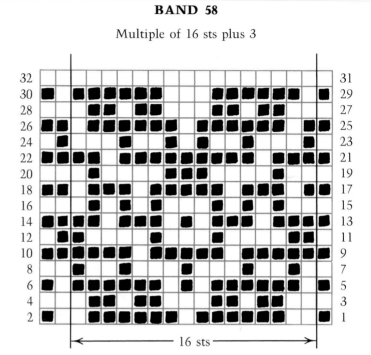

Figure 92

BAND 58

Multiple of 16 sts plus 3

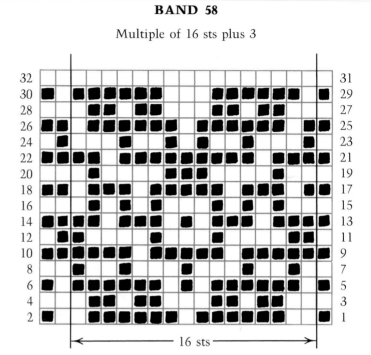

Figure 92. Top to bottom: Bands 58, 59, 60, 61, 62, 63, 64, 65, 66, 67, 68, 69, and 70

Figure 92

BAND 59

Multiple of 16 sts plus 3

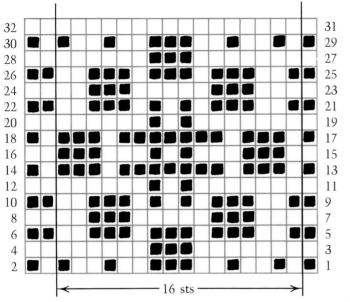

Figure 92

BAND 60

Multiple of 18 sts plus 3

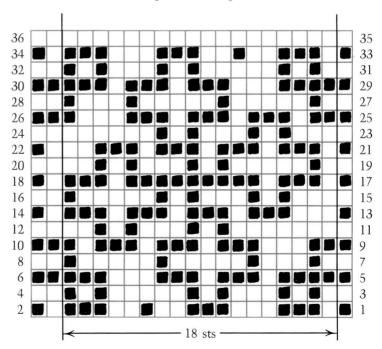

Figure 92

BAND 61

Multiple of 18 sts plus 3

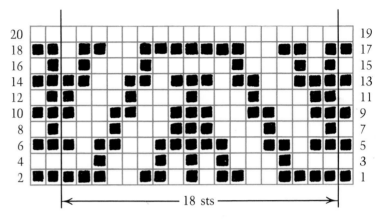

Figure 92

BAND 62

Multiple of 10 sts plus 3

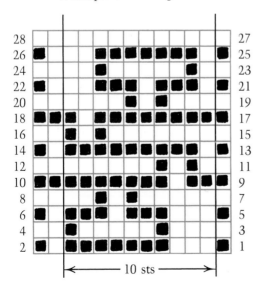

Figure 92

BAND 63

Multiple of 14 sts plus 3

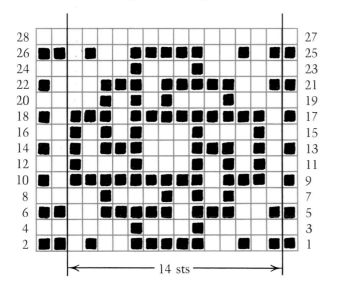

14 sts

Figure 92

BAND 64

Multiple of 12 sts plus 3

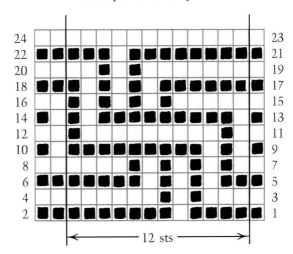

12 sts

Figure 92

BAND 65

Multiple of 18 sts plus 3

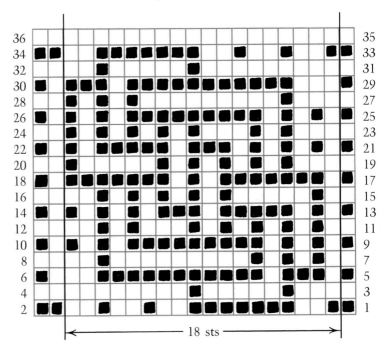

← 18 sts →

Figure 92

BAND 66

Multiple of 20 sts plus 3

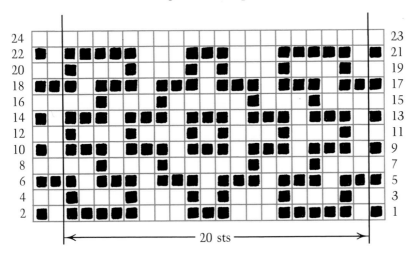

← 20 sts →

Figure 92

BAND 67

Multiple of 20 sts plus 3

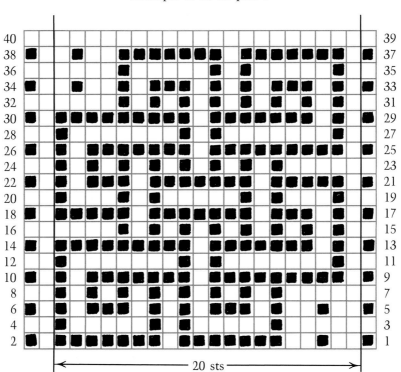

20 sts

Figure 92

BAND 68: "Buckle"

Multiple of 20 sts plus 3

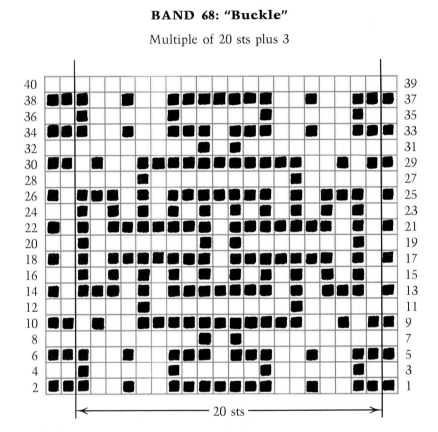

20 sts

Figure 92

BAND 69

Multiple of 10 sts plus 3

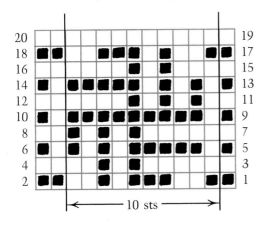

Figure 92

BAND 70

Multiple of 20 sts plus 3

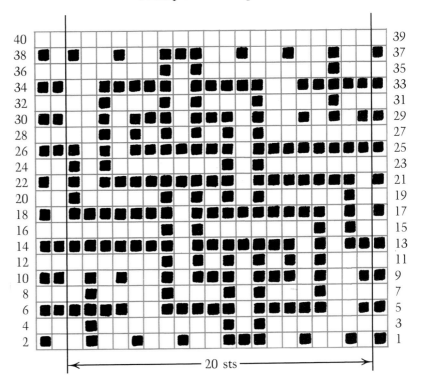

Figure 93

BAND 71

Multiple of 16 sts plus 3

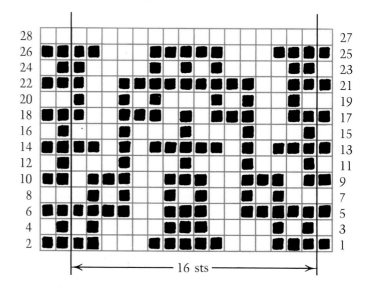

16 sts

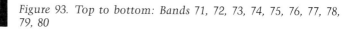

Figure 93. Top to bottom: Bands 71, 72, 73, 74, 75, 76, 77, 78, 79, 80

Figure 93

BAND 72

Multiple of 24 sts plus 3

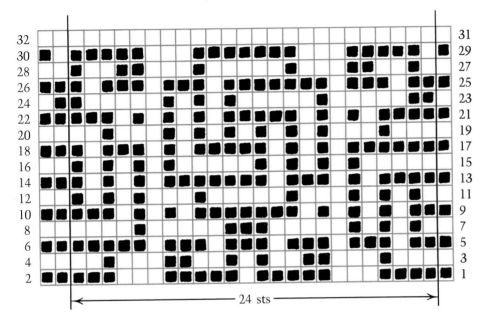

24 sts

Figure 93

BAND 73

Multiple of 16 sts plus 3

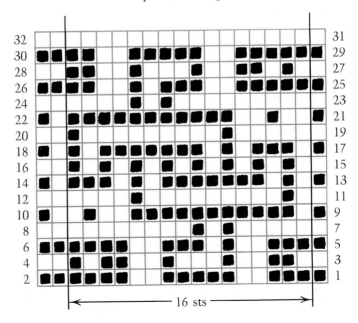

16 sts

Figure 93

BAND 74

Multiple of 16 sts plus 3

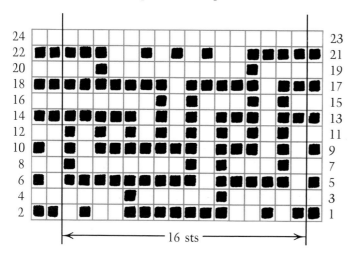

Figure 93

BAND 75

Multiple of 18 sts plus 3

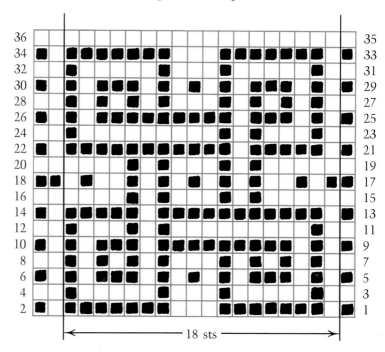

Figure 93

BAND 76

Multiple of 20 sts plus 3

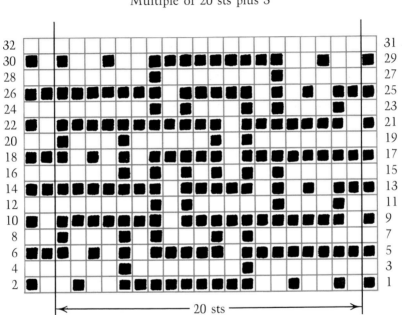

20 sts

Figure 93

BAND 77

Multiple of 24 sts plus 3

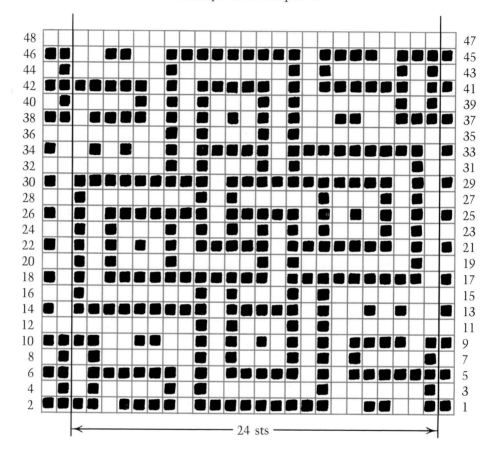

24 sts

Figure 93

BAND 78

Multiple of 24 sts plus 3

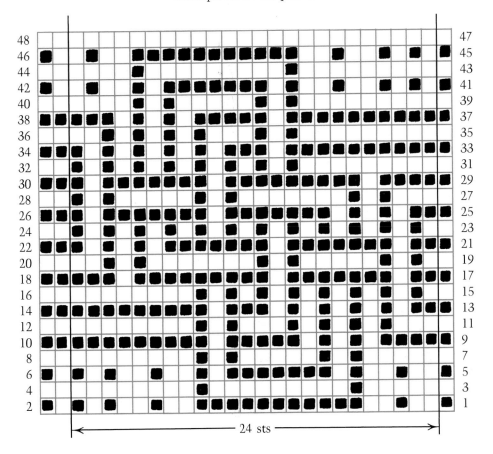

24 sts

Figure 93

BAND 79

Multiple of 18 sts plus 3

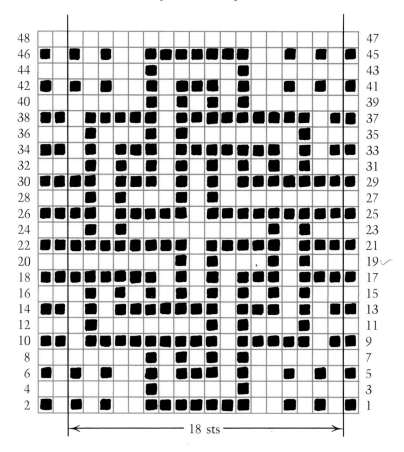

Figure 93

BAND 80

Multiple of 24 sts plus 3

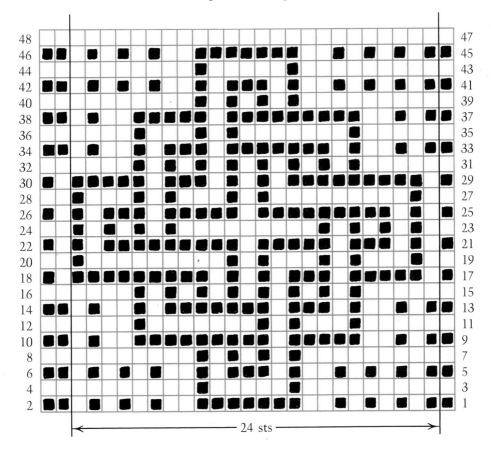

24 sts

Figure 94. Top to bottom: Bands 81, 82, 83, 84, 85, 86, 87, 88, 89, and 90

Figure 94

BAND 81

Multiple of 16 sts plus 3

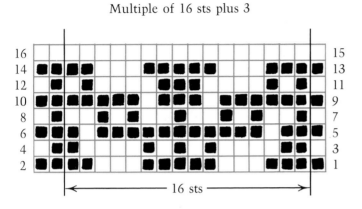

Figure 94

BAND 82

Multiple of 12 sts plus 3

(for an all-over mosaic pattern, work Rows 5–28 only)

Figure 94

BAND 83

Multiple of 16 sts plus 3

(for an all-over mosaic pattern, work Rows 9–40 only)

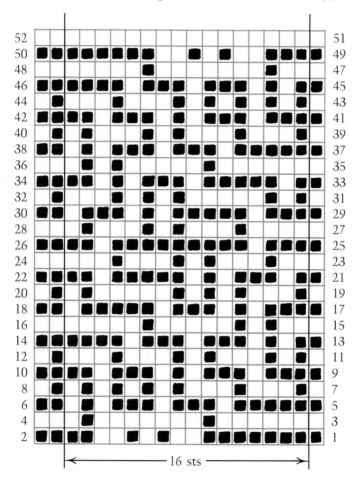

Figure 94

BAND 84

Multiple of 10 sts plus 3

(for an all-over mosaic pattern,
work Rows 5–24 only)

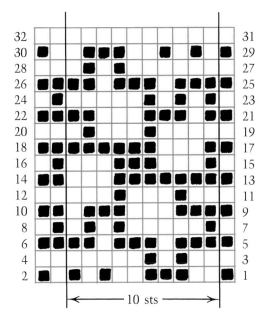

← 10 sts →

Figure 94

BAND 85

Multiple of 18 sts plus 3

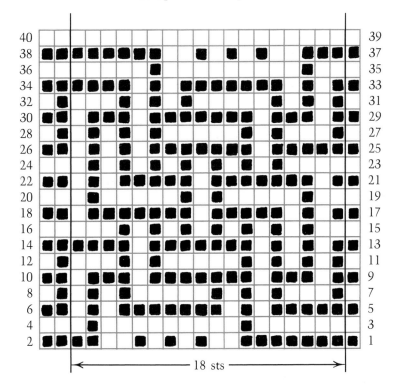

← 18 sts →

Figure 94

BAND 86

Multiple of 20 sts plus 3

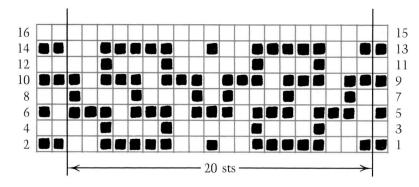

BAND 87

Figure 94

Multiple of 12 sts plus 3

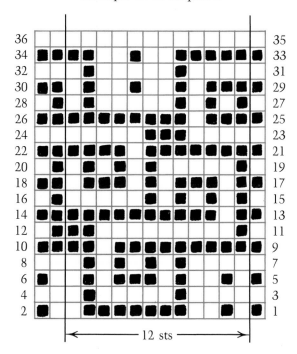

Figure 94

BAND 88

Multiple of 18 sts plus 3

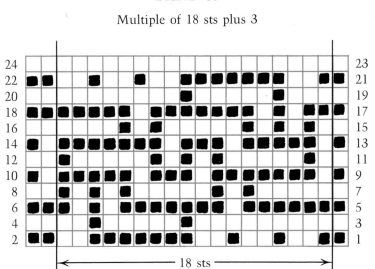

Figure 94

BAND 90

Multiple of 10 sts plus 3

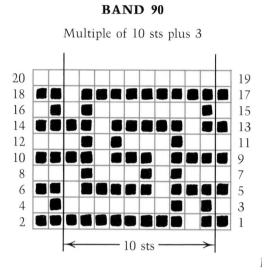

← 10 sts →

Figure 94

BAND 89

Multiple of 22 sts plus 3

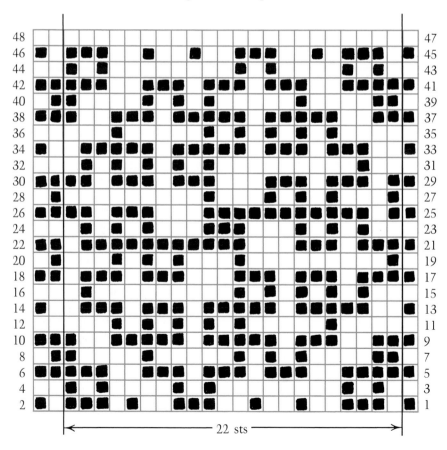

← 22 sts →

3

SHADOW PATTERNS

Here is a new term, coined to describe a new and fascinating class of mosaic patterns. Each shadow mosaic design consists of a black motif upside down, interlocking with and alternating with the *same* motif in white, right side up. These contrasting patterns interlock with each other in a multitude of interesting ways, and lend themselves to several different interpretations, which can be varied at the knitter's whim. Whichever method of interpretation you choose, your shadow mosaic designs will look the same upside down and right side up, and will "shadow" each other in clever and intriguing shapes.

Method I—Color Reversal

Each shadow mosaic chart shows an *odd* number of 2-row stripes. It begins with a row of black squares at the bottom, as usual, and ends with another row of black squares at the top. These final black rows are always worked straight across, without slip-stitches; so the chart shows no white squares on its top line.

The color-reversal method of following such a chart goes like this. Cast on and work the first preliminary white row as usual. Follow the chart through its pattern rows, ending with 2 black rows worked straight across. For the next repeat of the pattern rows, reverse the colors. Start again at Row 1 using black squares to represent *light* yarn, and white squares to represent *dark* yarn. Thus the straight rows at the top of this second repeat will be light, not dark. Make the third repeat just like the first, then reverse colors again to make the fourth repeat like the second. The pattern proceeds up the fabric in a series of bands with each color alternately switching from black squares to white squares.

This method is shown in most of the sample photographs. To see the

151

startlingly different designs that can be created from each pattern with other methods, you'll have to try them for yourself!

Method II—Pattern Reversal

In this method you don't reverse colors; you reverse the pattern rows instead. After going once through these rows in the order shown on the chart, ending with the last 2 black rows, work *backward* down the chart from top to bottom, beginning with the first white row under the top line, then the next black row under that, then the next white row under that, and so on. In other words, if the chart shows a total of 14 pattern rows, the reversed order of the second repeat is: Rows 11–12, Rows 9–10, Rows 7–8, Rows 5–6, Rows 3–4, Rows 1–2. Having come back to the bottom of the chart, *work 2 plain rows* without slip-stitches in the *light* yarn. This corresponds to the light line of your cast-on and preliminary row, and prepares you to start up the chart again with the rows in normal order for the third repeat. Continue in this manner, alternating normal order and reverse order of the rows every time you begin a fresh band of pattern.

Method II changes the whole design of a shadow mosaic. For instance, a pattern that forms chevrons when worked by Method I will form, instead, diamonds when worked by Method II. More complex patterns will shift themselves into many delightful surprises for you. Each shadow mosaic has its own unique pattern-reversal shape, which you will see only when you have worked the pattern by this method.

Method III—Multicolor Reversal

Shadow mosaics lend themselves beautifully to pattern knitting in bands of more than two colors. Each complete design of each color interlocks in its first half with the color below, and in its second half with the color above. This lively arrangement is very simply accomplished by carrying each color twice through the charted pattern rows, the first time on the black squares, the second time on the white squares.

Let's assume that you want to work a shadow pattern in continuous bands of 5 different colors, A, B, C, D, and E. Cast on with A and work the preliminary row. Join B, to begin at the first row at the bottom of the chart.

> * *First repeat*—Use B for black squares, A for white squares. Break A, join C.
>
> *Second repeat*—Use C for black squares, B for white squares. Break B, join D.
>
> *Third repeat*—Use D for black squares, C for white squares. Break C, join E.
>
> *Fourth repeat*—Use E for black squares, D for white squares. Break D, join A.
>
> *Fifth repeat*—Use A for black squares, E for white squares. Break E, join B.
>
> Repeat in this same order from *.

This method makes a fascinating way to use up leftover odds and ends of variously colored yarn. It creates unusual and beautiful garments, afghans, stoles, wall hangings, and other mosaic articles. The more strongly contrasting the colors, the better. Be sure that any two colors you place in contact with each other will provide enough contrast to show the figures of the pattern.

Method IV—Multicolor Pattern Reversal

This method combines elements of Methods II and III. Use any number of different colors, carrying each color twice through the pattern rows, as in Method III; but reverse the order of the pattern rows (instead of reversing colors) in every other repeat, as in Method II. Thus if a color starts out on the black squares, it remains on the black squares throughout 2 repeats instead of switching to white squares the second time through the pattern.

If a color starts out on the white squares, it remains on the white squares throughout 2 repeats. But you still change *one* of the colors each time you restart the pattern, either forward or backward.

It isn't necessary to remember any particular sequence for this. All you have to do is assign each new color to whichever squares—black or white—are not already occupied by the second repeat of the other color.

Method V–Decorative Bands

If one of the two colors in a shadow mosaic is worked alone for a number of rows before and after the pattern, it takes on the aspect of a background color. The contrasting color worked in the pattern therefore makes a decorative band across this background. Such a decorative band should contain at least 2 repeats of the pattern rows, either color-reversed or pattern-reversed, so the design will be symmetrical upward and downward. A second or third color, 2 repeats of each, may be added to the band to enhance the "shadow" effect. Many different shadow mosaics may be used in the same project, several repeats at a time, to cover the entire surface of the fabric with interesting designs while the background color forms a bridge from one pattern to the next. Some of the garments shown in this book are developed by this method, so you can see examples of the sparkling effects it can produce.

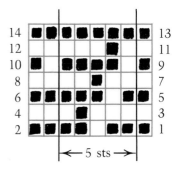

Figure 95

SHADOW 1

Multiple of 5 sts plus 3

Figure 95. Shadow 1

Figure 96

SHADOW 2

Multiple of 6 sts plus 3

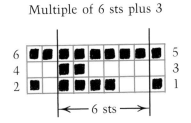

Figure 96

SHADOW 3

Multiple of 12 sts plus 3

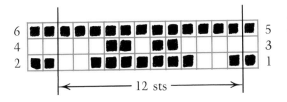

Figure 96.
Above: Shadow 2; below: Shadow 3

Figure 97

SHADOW 4

Multiple of 6 sts plus 3

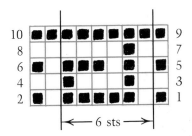

Figure 97. Shadow 4

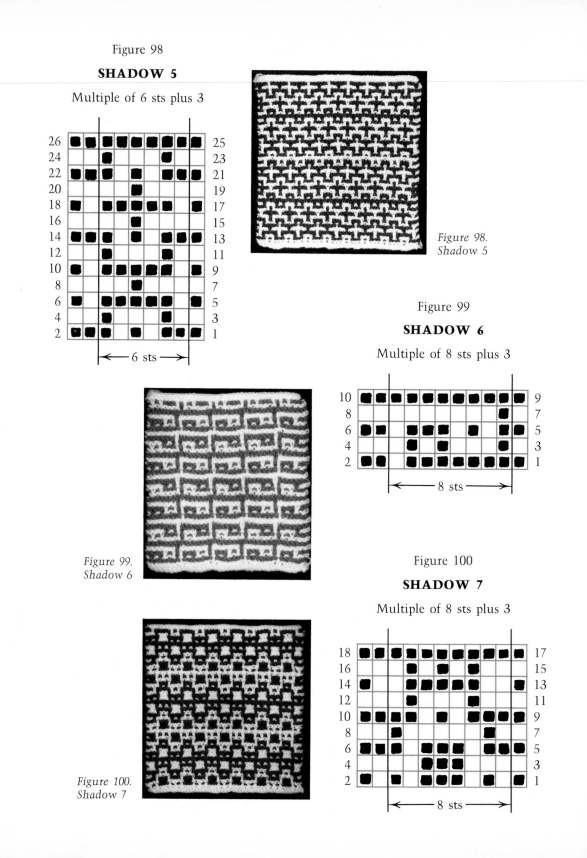

Figure 98

SHADOW 5

Multiple of 6 sts plus 3

←— 6 sts —→

Figure 98.
Shadow 5

Figure 99.
Shadow 6

Figure 99

SHADOW 6

Multiple of 8 sts plus 3

←— 8 sts —→

Figure 100

SHADOW 7

Multiple of 8 sts plus 3

Figure 100.
Shadow 7

←——— 8 sts ———→

Figure 101

SHADOW 8

Multiple of 8 sts plus 3

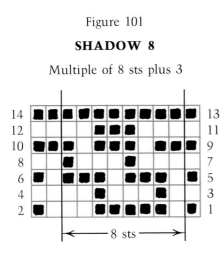

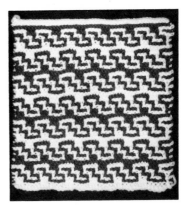

Figure 101. Shadow 8

Figure 102

SHADOW 9

Multiple of 10 sts plus 3

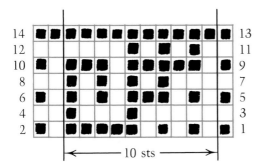

Figure 102. Shadow 9

Figure 103

SHADOW 10

Multiple of 10 sts plus 3

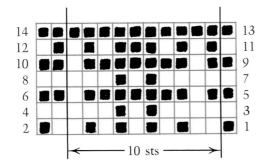

Figure 103. Shadow 10

Figure 104

SHADOW 11

Multiple of 10 sts plus 3

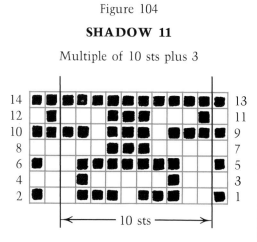

Figure 104. Shadow 11

Figure 105. Shadow 12

Figure 105

SHADOW 12

Multiple of 10 sts plus 3

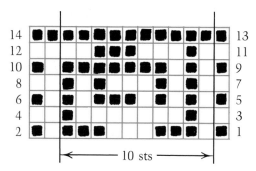

Figure 106

SHADOW 13

Multiple of 10 sts plus 3

Figure 106. Shadow 13

Figure 107. Shadow 14

Figure 107

SHADOW 14

Multiple of 10 sts plus 3

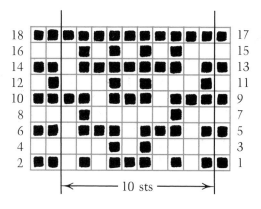

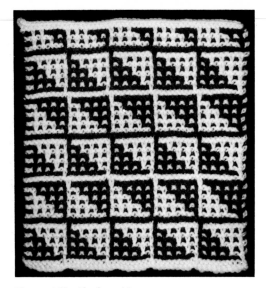

Figure 108. Shadow 15

Figure 108

SHADOW 15

Multiple of 10 sts plus 3

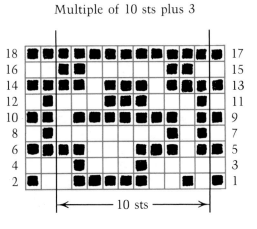

Figure 109. Shadow 16

Figure 109

SHADOW 16

Multiple of 10 sts plus 3

Figure 110

SHADOW 17

Multiple of 10 sts plus 3

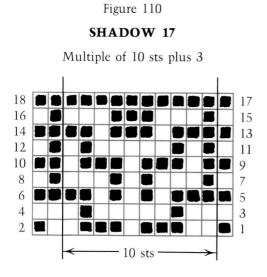

Figure 110. Shadow 17

Figure 111. Shadow 18

Figure 111

SHADOW 18

Multiple of 10 sts plus 3

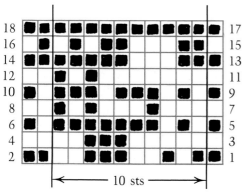

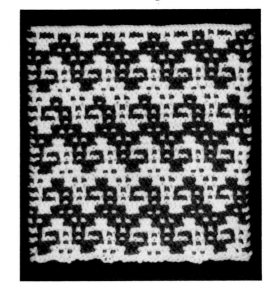

Figure 112. Shadow 19

Figure 112

SHADOW 19

Multiple of 10 sts plus 3

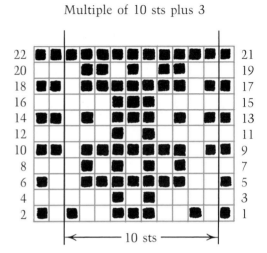

Figure 113. Shadow 20

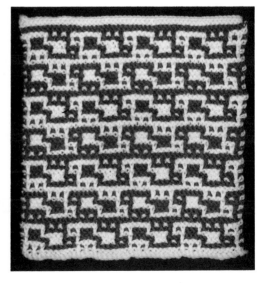

Figure 113

SHADOW 20

Multiple of 12 sts plus 3

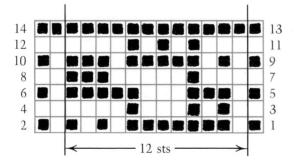

Figure 114

SHADOW 21

Multiple of 12 sts plus 3

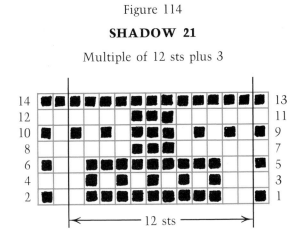

Figure 114. Shadow 21

Figure 115. Shadow 22

Figure 115

SHADOW 22

Multiple of 12 sts plus 3

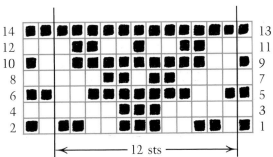

Figure 116

SHADOW 23

Multiple of 12 sts plus 3

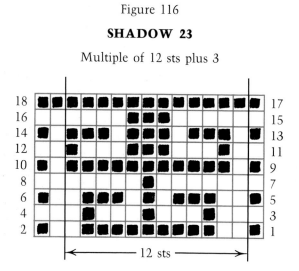

12 sts

Figure 116. Shadow 23

Figure 117. Shadow 24

Figure 117

SHADOW 24

Multiple of 12 sts plus 3

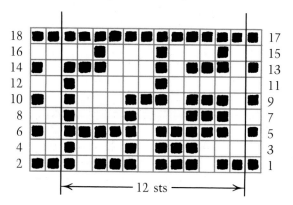

12 sts

Figure 118

SHADOW 25

Multiple of 12 sts plus 3

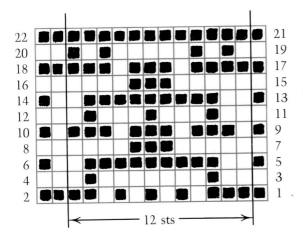

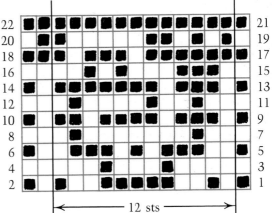

Figure 118. Shadow 25

Figure 119. Shadow 26

Figure 119

SHADOW 26

Multiple of 12 sts plus 3

Figure 120

SHADOW 27

Multiple of 12 sts plus 3

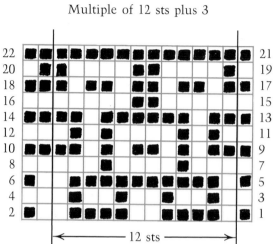

Figure 120. Shadow 27

Figure 121. Shadow 28

Figure 121

SHADOW 28

Multiple of 14 sts plus 3

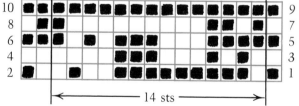

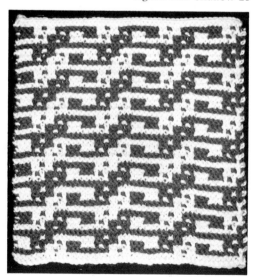

Figure 122

SHADOW 29

Multiple of 14 sts plus 3

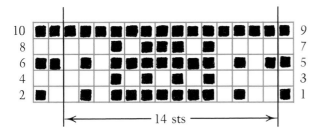

Figure 122. Shadow 29

Figure 123

SHADOW 30

Multiple of 14 sts plus 3

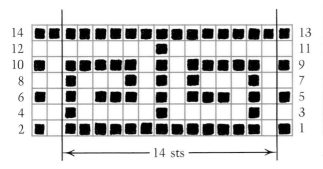

Figure 123. Shadow 30

Figure 124

SHADOW 31

Multiple of 14 sts plus 3

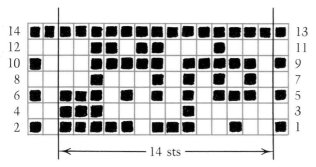

Figure 124. Shadow 31

Figure 125. Shadow 32

Figure 125

SHADOW 32

Multiple of 14 sts plus 3

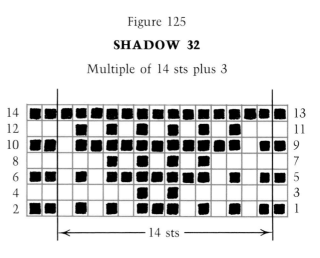

14 sts

Figure 126. Shadow 33

Figure 126

SHADOW 33

Multiple of 14 sts plus 3

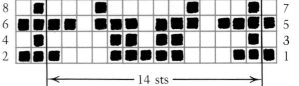

14 sts

Figure 127

SHADOW 34

Multiple of 14 sts plus 3

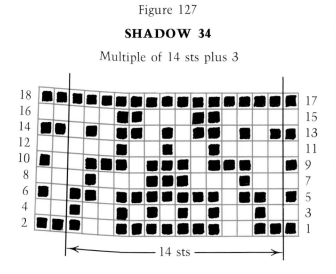

14 sts

Figure 127

SHADOW 35

Multiple of 14 sts plus 3

14 sts

Figure 127. Above: Shadow 34; below: Shadow 35; both worked in a straight-strip potholder ready for folding and sewing

Figure 128. Shadow 36

Figure 128

SHADOW 36

Multiple of 14 sts plus 3

Figure 129. Shadow 37

Figure 129

SHADOW 37

Multiple of 14 sts plus 3

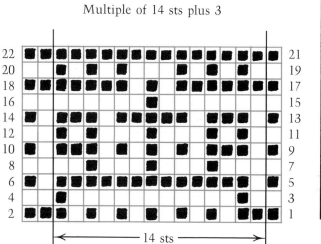

Figure 130

SHADOW 38

Multiple of 14 sts plus 3

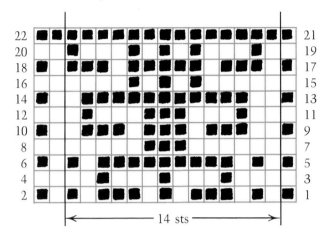

Figure 130. Shadow 38

Figure 131. Shadow 39

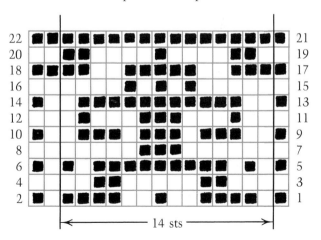

Figure 131

SHADOW 39

Multiple of 14 sts plus 3

Figure 132

SHADOW 40

Multiple of 14 sts plus 3

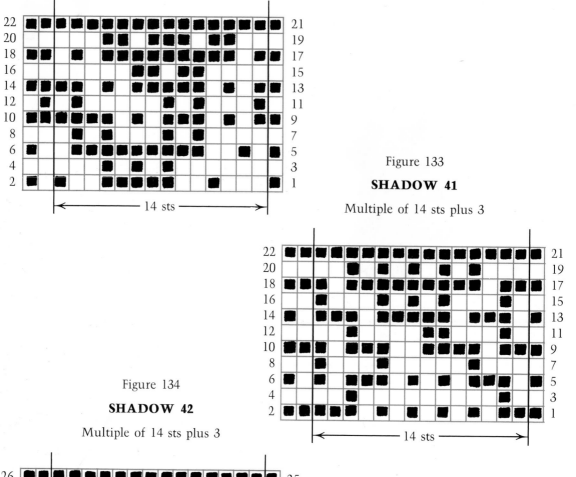

Figure 133

SHADOW 41

Multiple of 14 sts plus 3

Figure 134

SHADOW 42

Multiple of 14 sts plus 3

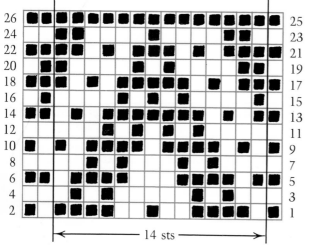

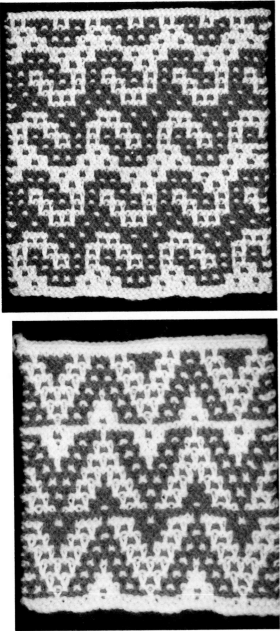

Figure 132. Shadow 40

Figure 133. Shadow 41

Figure 134. Shadow 42

Figure 135

SHADOW 43

Multiple of 14 sts plus 3

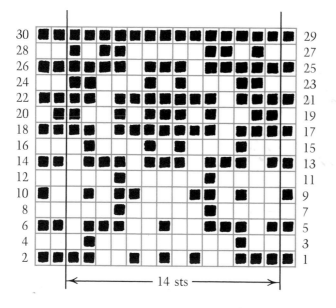

Figure 135. Shadow 43

Figure 136

SHADOW 44

Multiple of 14 sts plus 3

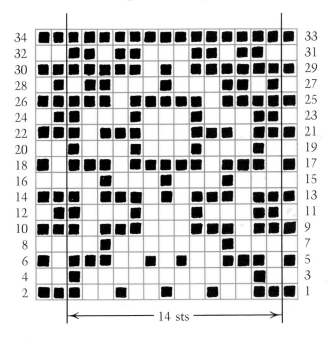

Figure 136. Shadow 44

Figure 137

SHADOW 45

Multiple of 16 sts plus 3

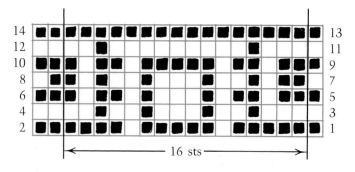

Figure 137. Shadow 45

Figure 138. Shadow 46

Figure 138

SHADOW 46

Multiple of 16 sts plus 3

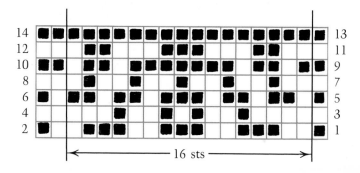

Figure 139

SHADOW 47

Multiple of 16 sts plus 3

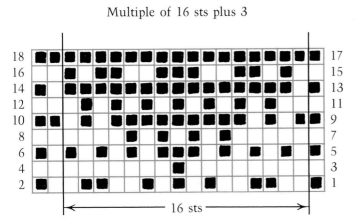

Figure 139. Shadow 47

Figure 140

SHADOW 48

Multiple of 16 sts plus 3

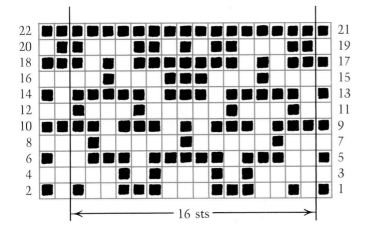

Figure 140. Shadow 48

Figure 141

SHADOW 49

Multiple of 16 sts plus 3

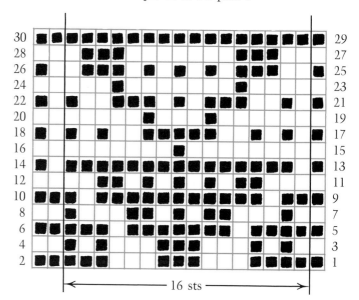

Figure 141. Shadow 49

Figure 142

SHADOW 50

Multiple of 18 sts plus 3

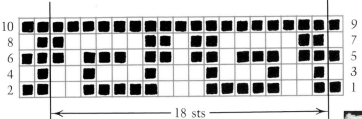

Figure 142. Shadow 50

Figure 143. Shadow 51

Figure 143

SHADOW 51

Multiple of 18 sts plus 3

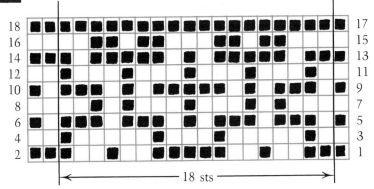

Figure 144

SHADOW 52

Multiple of 18 sts plus 3

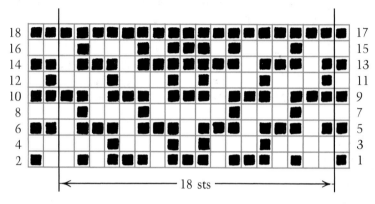

Figure 144.
Shadow 52

Figure 145

SHADOW 53

Multiple of 18 sts plus 3

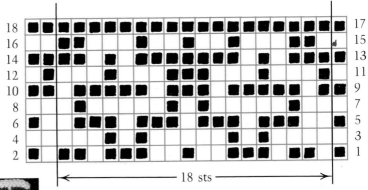

Figure 145.
Shadow 53

Figure 146

SHADOW 54

Multiple of 18 sts plus 3

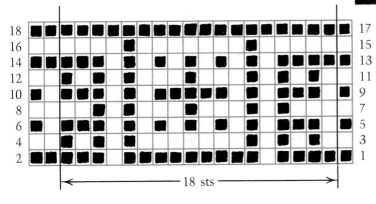

Figure 146.
Shadow 54

Figure 147

SHADOW 55

Multiple of 18 sts plus 3

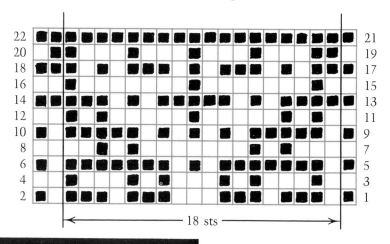

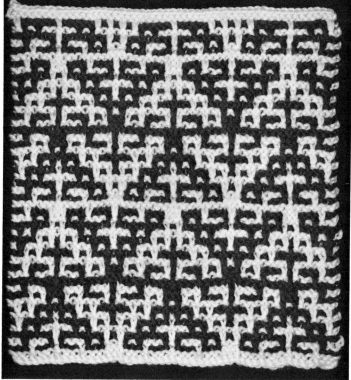

Figure 147. Shadow 55

Figure 148

SHADOW 56

Multiple of 18 sts plus 3

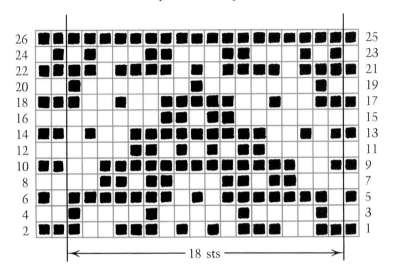

Figure 148. Shadow 56

Figure 149

SHADOW 57

Multiple of 20 sts plus 3

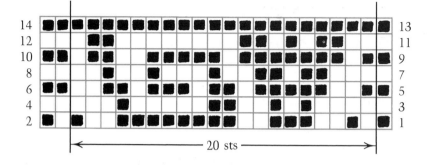

Figure 150

SHADOW 58

Multiple of 22 sts plus 3

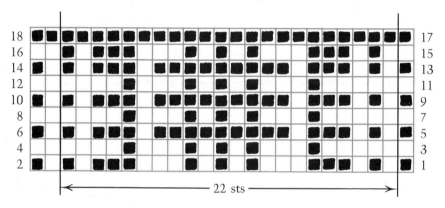

Figure 151

SHADOW 59

Multiple of 22 sts plus 3

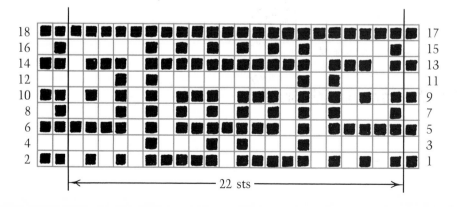

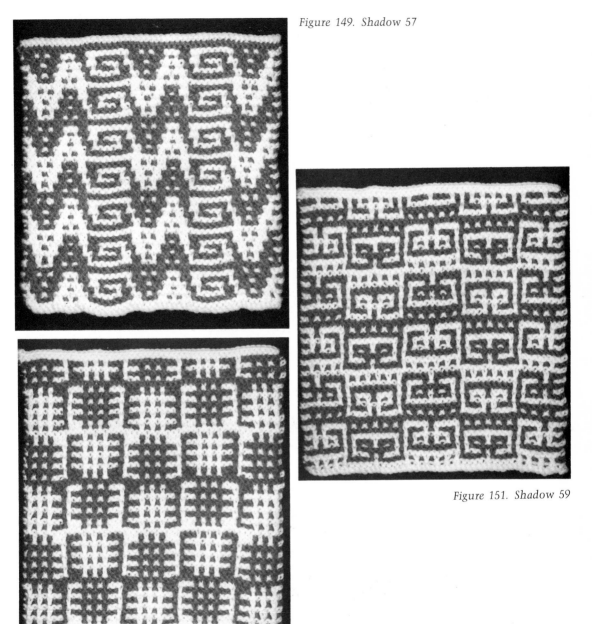

Figure 149. Shadow 57

Figure 151. Shadow 59

Figure 150. Shadow 58

Figure 152

SHADOW 60

Multiple of 22 sts plus 3

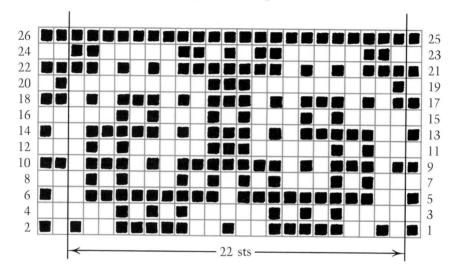

Figure 153

SHADOW 61

Multiple of 26 sts plus 3

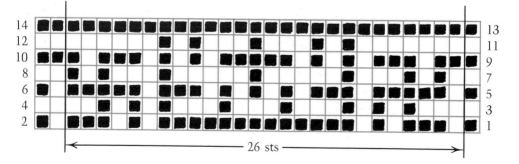

Figure 154

SHADOW 62

Multiple of 26 sts plus 3

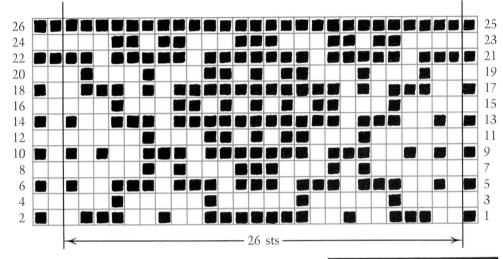

26 sts

Figure 152. Shadow 60

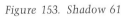

Figure 153. Shadow 61

Figure 154. Shadow 62

Figure 155

SHADOW 63

Multiple of 30 sts plus 3

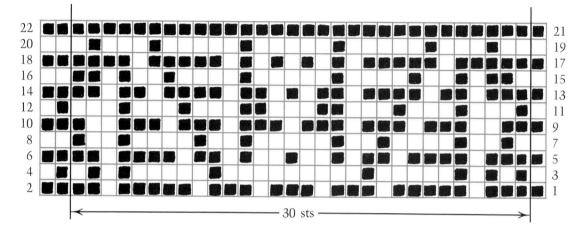

30 sts

Figure 155. Shadow 63

Figure 156. Shadow 64

Figure 156

SHADOW 64

Multiple of 30 sts plus 3

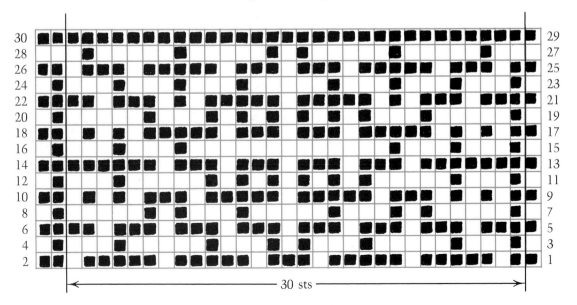

Figure 157

SHADOW 65

Multiple of 26 sts plus 3

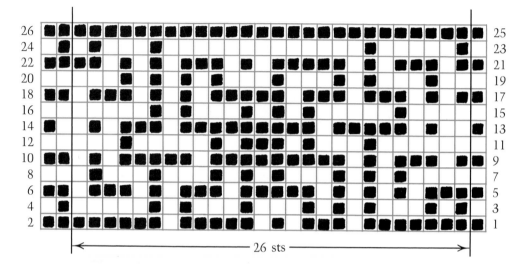

Figure 157. Shadow 65

4

DESIGNING WITH MOSAIC PATTERNS

Beginner's Straight-Strip Projects:

STOLE, SCARF, WALL HANGING, PILLOW COVER, BABY BLANKET, RUG, TWO-STRIP PONCHO
(Color 1, Figures 158, 159, and 177)

Straight-strip projects are knitted articles that require no increase or decrease shaping. They are worked like sample swatches, by casting on a certain number of stitches and maintaining that same number on every row until a certain length is reached. Therefore any straight-strip item is a simple rectangle. The length-to-width proportions of such a rectangle may be varied at will, depending on the purpose for which it will be used.

STOLE

To begin any straight-strip project, first make a test swatch of your mosaic pattern with the yarn and needles that you intend to use for the project. On this swatch, measure your gauge (number of stitches to the inch). Multiply this gauge by the width that you want in the finished article. Then cast on this number of stitches.

A good width for a stole is about 20 inches. So if your gauge is 4 stitches to the inch, you'd cast on 4 x 20, or 80 stitches; if your gauge is 5 stitches to the inch, you'd cast on 5 x 20, or 100 stitches; if your gauge is 6 stitches to the inch, you'd cast on 6 x 20, or 120 stitches, and so on. Whatever number of stitches you use to begin, you simply maintain the same number throughout the entire length of 5 or 6 feet, or whatever length you wish, and bind off when the stole is long enough. You may change colors and/or patterns at will, anywhere along the way, for every mosaic pattern will work to the same gauge as long as the yarn and needle sizes do not change, and any mosaic pattern can be worked on any number of stitches.

191

Garter stitch is the best fabric type for a stole, because you'll want it to lie flat and keep its shape without curling at the edges; so plan on knitting, instead of purling, the wrong-side rows. When the stole is finished, you can tidy up the side edges, if you wish, with a row or two of single crochet. Place one sc in every other stripe along these edges. Cast-on and bound-off edges may be finished with fringe or tassels, or simply left plain.

SCARF

A scarf can be worked just like a stole, but smaller. A good proportion is a width of 6" or 7" to a length of 1 to 1½ yards. Use a fine, soft yarn, such as baby wool, and small needles. A single-thickness scarf in a garter-stitch type of fabric may be lined with a length of thin silk or chiffon, if desired.

If you want a double-thick scarf with the right side of the pattern facing out on both sides, you may use a stockinette-stitch fabric and begin with twice the desired width. When the strip is long enough, bind off, fold it in half lengthwise, and sew the side edges together. Another way to make a double-thick scarf is to knit two strips separately and sew them together back to back. In this case, it is a pleasant idea to reverse the colors, making the pattern positive (dark-on-light) on one strip, and negative (light-on-dark) on the other. Of course, a third way to make a double-thick scarf—without any sewing—is to work it as a seamless tube on a small (16") circular needle, instead of as a strip on straight needles.

WALL HANGING

If it ever happens that you begin a stole or a scarf, and run out of either yarn or patience before it has attained the necessary length, don't bother to rip out the work—hang it on the wall instead! A mosaic-patterned wall hanging can be any width, from a narrow 4- or 5-inch bell-pull size to a yard wide; or any length, from 1 to 1½ feet to a dramatic floor-to-ceiling sweep of color. It's a wonderful way to use up odds and ends of varicolored yarns in a decorative conversation piece. You can even plan your room decor around it, adding mosaic pillows, throw rugs, and afghans to match.

Of course you'll want to work a garter-stitch fabric in a wall hanging, so it won't curl at the sides. If you wish, you can sew on a lining or backing of heavy poplin or canvas, to minimize stretching. Leave an inch or two open between the knitting and the backing fabric at the upper corners, to insert a rod. An unlined hanging can be attached to its rod by means of a casing, which you make by knitting a plain piece 2 or 3 inches long at the top; turn this under to the back and sew it in place, forming a small tunnel for the rod to pass through.

The lower edge can be finished with fringe, tassels, an edging, or a second casing for a bottom rod. Materials for a wall hanging also offer several creative choices. Ordinary knitting yarns in wool or synthetic fibers should be worked tightly, on small needles, so the fabric will be firm. You could also use less elastic material, such as linen or cotton yarns, or several strands of crochet cotton, or rug yarn, or twine, or any fancy cord that is pliable enough for knitting. Metallic yarns, too, will give sparkling effects.

PILLOW COVER (Straight-Strip Bag)

Measure the width of the pillow that you intend to cover, multiply by your stitch gauge, cast on the resulting number of stitches and begin a strip. Knit until the strip is twice as long as the pillow. Fold the strip at the halfway point, sew or crochet the side edges together, and insert a zipper between the cast-on and bound-off edges. That's all! The basic pillow is finished. You may add refinements—linings, fringes, tassels—to improve your pillow if you wish. Incidentally, a lined pillow cover with the further addition of a pair of handles make a delightful mosaic tote bag. Knit or crocheted cords, thin strips with ribbon lining, or several strands of heavy household twine braided together will make such handles.

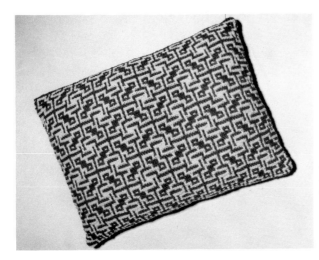

Figure 158. Straight-strip pillow cover worked in Mosaic 86

BABY BLANKET

A crib or carriage blanket should be about a yard wide and a yard and a half long. Multiply your stitch guage by the desired width, cast on, and work a cheerful combination of colors and patterns to the desired length. This is another opportunity to use up leftover yarns: the more colors, the gayer the result. Remember, babies like bright colors. Side edges may be finished with single crochet, as for the stole, or left plain. To work a wide strip comfortably, knit back and forth in rows on a 29″ or 36″ circular needle instead of using the shorter straight needles.

If your baby blanket is still in good shape after the last baby has outgrown it, you can always convert it into a wall hanging!

RUG

Mosaic patterns go well with heavy rug yarn and large needles to make a decorative bath mat, hearth mat, or throw rug. Following standard procedure, take the stitch gauge from a test swatch and multiply by the desired width to determine the number of stitches to be cast on. Work to the desired length and bind off. If the rug is to be laid on a bare floor, add a nonskid backing of rubberized fabric or spray. For a bath mat, you might use a backing of terrycloth. Finish side edges with rug binding or with crochet or with a knitted border, made as follows:

With a long needle, pick up stitches along one edge of the rectangle from corner to corner. (If it is a cast-on or bound-off edge, pick up 1 stitch from each cast-on or bound-off stitch; if it is a side edge, pick up one stitch from each 2-row stripe.) Work a mosaic band pattern back and forth in rows, beginning with a plain knit row on the wrong side. Increase 1 stitch at each side—that is, in each corner—every other row. Finish with 2 plain knit rows and bind off on right side, knitting all stitches. Repeat this border band on each of the other 3 edges of the rug. Weave mitered increased corners together.

You can also work this same kind of border all at once on a long circular needle, by picking up stitches from all edges of the rectangle, placing markers at each corner, and working in rounds. Begin with a plain purl round and remember to increase 1 stitch each side of each corner marker every other round. This saves the trouble of weaving the mitered corners together. If your rug is large and heavy, though, you may not be able to fit all the stitches required for a knit border on one circular needle. In this case, use three or four of them, passing from one to the next as when knitting a small tube on sock needles; or else knit the border one edge at a time, as given above.

TWO-STRIP PONCHO

A very easy way of constructing a poncho is to knit 2 identical straight strips and fasten them together end-to-side. Thus the 2 strips hang on the bias, back and front, to make a strikingly designed garment.

For an average size, begin the first strip by casting on enough stitches to make a width of about 25 inches. Work in mosaic patterns until the piece is a yard long. Don't bind off. Break the yarn, leaving a long end for later sewing, and place the stitches on a holder or a length of string. Work the second strip exactly like the first. Join them together in the following manner.

With right sides facing you, lay the top end of piece 1 against the left side of piece 2, flush with the lower left-hand corner of piece 2. With the long yarn end, sew the loose stitches of piece 1 off their holder or string onto the side edge of piece 2, matching each stitch with one 2-row stripe. When you come to the end of the stitches, you should have 10 or 11 inches of the side edge of piece 2 remaining unsewed; this will form a hole for the neck. Turn to the other side, and attach the top end of piece 2 to the left side edge of piece 1 in the same way. There's your poncho—the simplest garment shape imaginable, but elegant and original withal.

To make a border for the lower edges of the garment, pick up stitches all around these edges on a long circular needle, placing a marker on the needle at each of the 2 points, front and back. Purl 1 round, then work a mosaic band pattern, increasing 1 stitch on each side of each marker every other round. It's a good idea to arrange your pattern so that it increases symmetrically on each side of each marker, by matching pattern lines at these points. Finish with a plain knit round, then a plain purl round, and bind off.

Instead of a knit border on picked-up stitches, you may choose to finish your poncho with fringe or with a knit or crocheted edging, or just leave the lower edges alone. Any version of the simple 2-strip poncho is fun to knit and fun to wear.

*Figure 159. Two-strip poncho worked in Bands 1–13,
with a border of Band 18*

Sampler Squares:
Afghans, Potholders, and Others

(Color 2, Figures 24, 50, 61–63, 127, 160, 161)

If you're the kind of knitter who enjoys doing many different patterns in fairly rapid succession, you can have fun making articles out of sampler squares. The basic idea couldn't be easier: work a lot of squares, each with a different pattern and/or color combination, and sew them together. In other varieties of knitted fabrics, this ostensibly easy basic idea can lead to a number of nagging problems. More often than not, other varieties of knitted fabrics vary their stitch gauges from pattern to pattern, so you must constantly check each gauge separately, and change the stitch counts to get squares of the same size. All squares must be blocked to a standard size so they will fit together. Joining can be difficult, because one square may have more stitches and rows than an adjacent square, so you can't just match stitches or rows. Even length measurements can be tricky, plagued by decisions about when to bind off (now, or after one more row?).

But in mosaic knitting, every one of these problems is totally eliminated. Any mosaic pattern in the garter-stitch fabric style, when worked to exactly *twice* the number of rows as the number of stitches, will make a perfect square. Therefore you have only to count the 2-row stripes along the side edge of your piece; when you have as many of these stripes as the number of stitches cast on, your square is finished. Since mosaic patterns may be worked on any stitch count, regardless of pattern multiples, every square can have the same number of stitches and rows as every other, and all squares will automatically match in size—without any figuring, gauge-checking, or blocking. In fact, a project in mosaic sampler squares (despite its dazzling results) is a real beginner's project, requiring no pre-planning or calculation of any kind. Once you've decided on a number of stitches for the first square, and worked that square to twice that number of rows, there are no more decisions. You can work as many other squares as you want, in exactly the same way, confident that when you put them together they will all fit.

SAMPLER-SQUARE AFGHAN

Of course a mosaic afghan may be worked, like any other beginner's project, in straight strips. Several multipatterned strips of the same length, sewed together along their side edges, create a very good afghan. This requires less sewing than an afghan made of squares. But the nice thing about an afghan made of squares is that it can be constructed checkerboard-fashion, with adjacent squares laid alternately vertically and horizontally, so the finished article has a four-way stretch that retains its springiness and won't bag or sag. Joining the squares is a simple matter, too. Since each square has the same number of stitches as the number of 2-row stripes, you can attach each stitch of a cast-on or bound-off edge to each stripe in the *side* edge of an adjacent square. This makes a smooth, perfect joining without any guesswork, blocking, pinning, puckering, or stretching.

A sampler-square afghan can grow to any size, one square at a time. Leave a long tail of yarn at the corner of each cast-on and bound-off edge, and use these tails to sew your afghan squares together as each one is completed. As you practice more and more patterns in sampler squares, such an add-a-square afghan can grow with surprising swiftness to proportions generous enough to cover a king-size double bed, meanwhile disposing handsomely of all the leftover yarn scraps that you've been wanting to use up.

SQUARE POTHOLDER (Figure 127)

Sampler squares can be useful even if they aren't sewed together into an afghan. You (or your child who's just learning to knit) can brighten up your kitchen with a row of mosaic potholders. Take a heat-resistant yarn, such as cotton rug yarn, cast on enough stitches to make a width of about 8", and work any mosaic pattern until there are as many 2-row stripes as there are stitches. Add a backing of some plain cotton quilted fabric; overcast, blanket-stitch, or apply binding, if desired, around the edges, and sew a loop of cord or narrow tape to one corner. There's your new potholder, made in less time than it would take to go to the store and buy one—and the result is certainly much more original.

For a reversible mosaic potholder, make 2 squares and sew them together back to back, with the lining of quilted fabric in between. This design

Figure 160. Sampler-square afghan in an assortment of mosaic and shadow patterns

Figure 161. Sampler-square poncho in an assortment of mosaic and shadow patterns, with a neckline border of Band 43

can be worked in one piece instead of two. After the first square is completed, knit a row or 2 of plain color, then begin a second pattern to make 2 continuous squares, or a rectangular strip twice as long as it is wide. Fold it across the center, insert the liner, and stitch or bind around the other three sides. Mosaic squares are pretty enough to come to the table, too, in varying roles such as hot-dish mats, place mats, trivets, or coasters. (See Figure 74 and Figure 127.)

SAMPLER-SQUARE PONCHO

For an easy, basic poncho design, make 48 mosaic squares, each approximately 6" or 7" in size. Sew them together checkerboard-fashion, like an afghan, in a large square with 7 small squares along each side, leaving out a single square in the very center for the neck opening. With a 16" circular needle, pick up stitches around this neck opening—1 picked-up stitch for each stitch or 2-row stripe—and place markers in each of the 4 corners. Work the neckband in rounds, in garter stitch (knit 1 round, then purl 1 round), making a double decrease in each corner every other round, until the neckband is wide enough. Bind off. A similar border can be worked all the way around the lower edges, if desired. Band patterns may be used instead of garter stitch for neck and lower borders.

This design is very flexible. The size of the squares can be varied, and so can the total number of squares. Just be sure that you have an odd number of squares along each side of the poncho, so the neck opening will be in the exact center. Also, be sure that the squares are big enough so that the omission of one of them will leave a hole large enough for the head to pass through. Otherwise, if you want to make a poncho of many tiny squares, you can use an even number along each side and omit 4 squares together in the center so the neck opening will be of a suitable size.

DROPPED-SHOULDER SWEATER

This primitive but attractive sweater shape is easily constructed of two rectangles of equal size, one for the front, and other for the back. Obviously it can be made of sampler squares sewed together as readily as of straight-knit pieces. Sew the 2 rectangles together at the shoulders, leaving a slot in the center for the neck, then pick up stitches across the upper corners for a pair of sleeves. Later, sew the entire side and sleeve seams at once, and add a narrow neckband to finish off the garment.

OTHER DESIGNS

Any rectangular article that might be designed as a straight strip can also be made of sewed-together sampler squares. If you have the foresight to make all your mosaic test swatches the same size as you learn different patterns—that is, each with the same number of stitches and twice that number of rows—you can put any amount of them together in different ways to make stoles, bags, pillow covers, crib blankets, scarves, wall hangings, and other things. Use up leftover bits of yarn to make mosaic squares in many colors, and sew them together any way you wish. Sampler squares are easily carried about, to be worked on in odd moments while you are traveling, or sitting on a beach, or waiting for a dental appointment, or attending a meeting, or letting your dinner "simmer slowly for one hour" according to the recipe. Keep a sampler-square-in-progress handy (in your big new mosaic-patterned tote bag) to go with you anywhere and fill in all those inevitable dull time-lapses with a useful, enjoyable, creative, and productive activity.

Bias Strips and Squares

(Color 3, Figures 162, 163, 164, 165, 166, and 167)

Bias shaping is a wonderful adventure for the novice knitter who is impatient to begin pattern work. In bias knitting, there's no need to make any preliminary decisions about yarn weights, needle sizes, stitch gauges, or numbers of stitches to cast on. A bias-knit strip or square begins at one corner, increases automatically until it is big enough for the desired purpose, then decreases automatically to the opposite corner. The shaping technique is always the same. Mosaic patterns lend an excitingly different effect to bias knitting as they slant across the piece at a 45-degree angle.

To begin a bias square, as for an afghan unit, mat, bag, potholder, or pillow cover, cast on 3 stitches and knit 1 row. On the next row, increase 1 stitch in each of the first and third stitches, to make a total of 5. Knit another row. On the next row, increase 1 stitch in each of the second and fourth stitches, to make a total of 7. Knit another row. Continue to work the garter-stitch fabric in this way, making 1 more stitch every other row in the second stitch from each side edge. The piece grows steadily, 2 stitches at a time, into a right-angled triangle. Tie on another color whenever you please, and begin to decorate the bias knitting with a mosaic pattern. When the triangle is as wide as you want it to be, start to *decrease* at the same rate—2 stitches every other row—at the side edges. Continue this until the piece narrows down to 3 final stitches. Work these last 3 stitches together, and the square is finished. Whatever its size or stitch gauge, the garter-stitch fabric ornamented with mosaic patterns will always make a perfect square; and any other square worked to the same total number of stitches with the same needles and yarn type will perfectly match the first.

To make a bias strip, as for a scarf, stole, wall hanging, baby blanket, or rectangular pillow cover, cast on 3 stitches and work an increasing triangle just like the square. When the triangle is wide enough, proceed with the straight part of the strip by increasing every other row at one side edge, and decreasing every other row at the other. Continue this until the strip is long enough. Then stop increasing, and decrease 1 stitch every other row at both side edges until the piece narrows down to the final 3 stitches and finishes, like the square, at the opposite corner.

Strips and squares in bias knitting are that simple. As long as you don't forget any of the increases or decreases along the way, your bias-knit piece enlarges, maintains its width, or diminishes with mechanical precision and regularity. Keeping the pattern(s) correct as the stitch count changes is also very simple once you have learned to read charts and to relate their black-and-white pictures to the color designs in your knitting.

It's easy to sew bias-knit strips and squares together to make larger projects such as afghans and blankets. There are no cast-on or bound-off edges. All edges are side edges, showing the neatly alternating stripes for easy row-by-row matching along the seams.

With the same simplicity, and freedom from preplanning, you can make 2 bias strips or squares at once, as for a bag or pillow constructed all in one piece. Cast on 2 stitches, with a marker between them. Knit 1 row. Increase 1 stitch in each stitch, to make 4. Knit another row. Increase 1 stitch in each stitch again, to make 8. Knit another row. Now continue to increase 4 stitches every other row, 1 in each stitch on either side of the marker, and 1 in each stitch next to the side edges. The marker remains in place to show the center of the piece, and the double square, or strip, develops outward from this center, forming a straight lower edge of 180 degrees. When the double square is wide enough, remove the marker and decrease each upper corner separately. When the double strip is wide enough but must be made longer, stop increasing at the side edges and decrease there instead, but continue the center increases on each side of the marker until the correct length is reached. Then divide the work and finish the 2 upper corners separately as for the square. To form the two sides of a bag or pillow cover, fold the piece along the center increase line and sew 2 of the open edges together, leaving the fourth edge free for a zipper insertion.

Figure 162. Double-bias bag, book, or pillow cover, two squares worked in a single piece with Mosaic 83 on one side, Mosaic 97 on the other

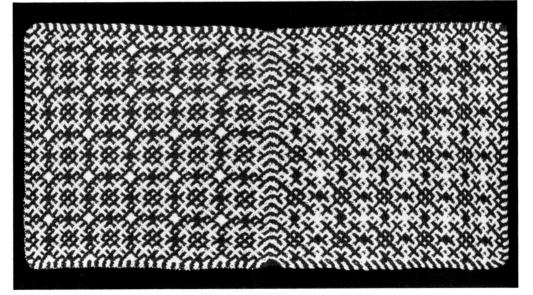

THE UNPLANNED BIAS-KNIT REVERSIBLE SWEATER

Bias-knit garments are intriguing. When you wear one, some fascinated but puzzled admirer usually will ask, "How on earth did you knit it slantwise?" Yet a bias-knit sweater with an uncomplicated shape is well within the ability of even a relatively inexperienced knitter. The classic crew-neck, dropped-shoulder pullover is easily made of two basic bias strips. This is a design that requires no calculation or preplanning at all. You can even omit the preliminary test swatch, since you don't have to check the stitch gauge. Directions apply to any stitch gauge and any size. You don't even have to take measurements in advance.

To make the first (front or back) piece, cast on 3 stitches and begin an increasing triangle as for the bias square. Lay out an old sweater of the correct width and compare it with your knitting. When one side of the increasing triangle is long enough to reach straight across the old sweater from one side seam to the other, stop increasing and start decreasing at the *right* side of the piece. Meanwhile, continue to increase at the left side, to form a bias strip. Work until the long side of the bias strip reaches all the way from the lower edge of the old sweater to the top of the shoulder. Then stop increasing, and begin decreasing both edges. Continue until all stitches are decreased away, and the strip is finished.

For the second (back or front) piece, make a reversed copy of the first. That is, when the triangle attains the right width, stop increasing and start decreasing at the *left* side of the piece. This makes the second bias strip slant in the opposite direction from the first, so the pattern rows will match exactly across shoulder and side seams when the two strips are sewed together. Sew the shoulder seams only, leaving an open slot in the center wide enough to pass the head through comfortably. Sleeves are made before the side seams are sewed, so the front, back, and sleeve edges can be joined in one continuous seam. Measure around the sleeve of the old sweater at the underarm. Mark this measurement on each side edge of your bias strips, half to one side, half to the other side, of the shoulder seam. With right side facing, pick up sleeve stitches between markers, 1 stitch from every 2-row stripe. Work the sleeve from these picked-up stitches downward to the wrist, decreasing as necessary. After you've worked 6 or 8 inches of sleeve, sew the side seam and continue sewing a little way down the sleeve, to make it easier to check sleeve length and width by trying the garment on as you go.

Figure 163. *Unplanned bias-knit reversible sweater, patterned with Bands 20, 24, 48, 62, 64, 65, 68, 70, 73, 74, and 76–79*

Figure 164. Unplanned double bias reversible sweater, showing the use of mosaic patterns in band form: Mosaics 1, 3, 12, 22, 25, 29, 35, 40, 43, 47, 59, 62–65, 70–73, 76, 77, 80, 83, 89, 92, and 99. Note matched and reversed patterning at center increase line

Figure 165. Unplanned double bias reversible sweater, back detail, with patterns different from those on the front, similarly matched at center increase line

Figure 166. Double-bias coat in Mosaics 10, 23, 33, 39, 60, and 74; Bands 29, 45, 47, 52, 57, 63, 84, 87, and 90; Shadows 12, 33, and 47

Figure 167. Double bias coat, back detail, showing matched and reversed patterning at sides and center increase line

To make a neckband, use double-pointed needles or a 16″ circular needle to pick up 1 stitch from every 2-row stripe around the neck slot. Work in garter stitch or some other border pattern until the neckband is the right width. Bind off. After the sleeves are finished and the back and front pieces sewed together at the sides, you can also make a border around the lower edge, using a 29″ circular needle to pick up one stitch from every 2-row stripe.

This is one of the easiest, but easily one of the most exciting, sweaters you'll ever knit. You may want to make it several times over, using different patterns and color combinations each time. Since you can use any mosaic patterns, any colors, any kind of yarn, any size needles, and any stitch gauge with the same directions for a garment of any size, from a small child's to a large man's, clearly this is a design that gives you all the fun of pattern work without the least bit of bother over measuring or fitting.

The same kind of sweater can be made of double bias strips, which is a pleasant way to use an assortment of band patterns because the bands will automatically form attractive chevrons. Begin at the center of back or front, and work upward and outward with the basic 4 increases (2 at the center, 1 each side) every other row until the width is correct. Then decrease at the sides, continuing to increase at the center, until the length is correct. Divide the knitting at the neck to finish the 2 bias strips separately out to the shoulder points. Pick up and knit the sleeves as directed above.

For maximum effectiveness in a garment made with double bias knitting, always match the patterns across the central increase line. This beautiful refinement also can be easily managed without preplanning, despite the fact that it *looks* as though every stitch of every row must have been counted and arranged very precisely from the center outward. All you really have to do is start the pattern at the right-hand edge at any point on its chart, and work along until you come to the central marker; after passing the marker, reverse the order of knit and slipped stitches that appear before the marker on the same row. Work each row the same way, keeping the pattern correct on both sides while the left-hand side is arranged in reverse, and the center will automatically produce symmetrically matched designs that add a masterful elegance to the whole creation.

Tabards

(Figure 168)

In medieval times, a tabard was a decorative overgarment worn by knights, heralds, pages, and other liveried personnel. The usual purpose of the tabard was to display heraldic colors, crests, or coats-of-arms, serving to identify the wearer in battle or on ceremonial occasions.

Today's knitter can use this time-honored style in exciting new ways, displaying patterns and color combinations in the inimitable medium of hand-created fabrics. A mosaic tabard looks marvelous over shirt-and-pants, swimsuits, little-girl dresses, or long, slim skirts. It can echo a color or colors from the rest of the outfit, for the modern put-together look. Best of all, it's the easiest thing in the world to knit. Like a straight stole, scarf, or wall hanging, it's composed of two identical unshaped strips—one for the front, the other for the back, joined together at the shoulders.

To start a tabard, make a test swatch of any mosaic pattern with the yarn and needles that you intend to use, and take the gauge (number of stitches to the inch). Multiply by the number of inches across your body from shoulder to shoulder. Cast on this many stitches and knit a straight piece, using one pattern throughout or a combination of patterns in contrasting bands. When the piece is long enough to reach below the hips, or any desired length, bind off. Add a fringe or edging if you wish. Work 1 row of single crochet along each side edge, or else pick up stitches along these edges for narrow knitted borders. In mosaic knitting it's very easy to pick up the right number of stitches for a border—all you have to do is pick up 1 stitch from each 2-row stripe.

Make a second piece just like the first. Sew the cast-on edges together for about 3″ in from each side, leaving an opening in the center for the neck. Attach four 8″ cords to the side edges at waistline level, to tie the front and back loosely together. Such cords can be made of matching yarn by twisting or braiding, or working a crochet chain, or casting on 8 inches of stitches and immediately binding them off, or knitting 3 stitches on a pair of double-pointed needles, always sliding the stitches to the other end of the needle instead of turning.

Figure 168. Two mosaic tabards, one shaped to points at lower edges, the other a straight strip fringed and patterned with Mosaics 3, 13, 19, 37, 42, 85, and 107; Bands 8 and 31

The bottom of each tabard piece may be given a pointed shape, if you prefer that to a straight edge. When the length has reached hipbone level, just decrease 1 stitch each side every other row until all but 2 or 3 stitches have been decreased away. Work these remaining stitches together, draw the yarn end through, and finish.

This simple but effective design gives you a wonderful opportunity to display your taste and skill in an original fashion that even a beginner can create without difficulty. Why not make several tabards, and mix-and-match them as you change the colors you wear underneath? You can have a lot of fun trying different mosaic patterns in this easy-to-make style.

Neckties

(Color 4, Figure 169)

A hand-knitted necktie is the most elegant of gifts, sure to be prized by the recipient for its comfort, durability, and originality. Since the only function of a necktie is to be decorative, and since individuality is the most important characteristic of any decorative accessory, it stands to reason that any man would be delighted to wear a necktie that is the only one of its kind in the world. Yet such a unique article is well within the grasp of any competent hand-knitter, and may be had for a very small expenditure of time, effort, and yarn.

Small needles (size 0 or size 1) and fine yarn (fingering yarn, dress yarn, or fine bouclé) are best for neckties. A tie can be knitted in a single thickness, or in a double thickness with a seam up the back, like most manufactured ties. In either case, it is knitted in five continuous sections, as follows:

Figure 169. Necktie worked in Mosaic 13

Section 1. Rapid increases (2 stitches increased every other row). These form the point at the lower end of the tie.

Section 2. Gradual decreases (2 stitches decreased every eighth row). These form the slowly tapering sides of the tie.

Section 3. Knitting even (no increases or decreases). This is the straight, narrow portion of the tie that passes around the collar.

Section 4. Gradual increases (2 stitches increased every eighth row). This is the slowly widening portion of the tie that leads to the second, narrower point.

Section 5. Rapid decreases (2 stitches decreased every other row). This is the final point, which reduces the width all the way down to one last stitch.

For the average tie, Section 1 covers about $2\frac{1}{2}''$ of length in a single thickness, or about 4" of length in a double thickness; Section 2 occupies 14" to 16"; Section 3 proceeds for about 17"; Section 4 makes another 9" or 10"; Section 5 is about 2" long for a single thickness, or 3" long for a double thickness. The total length can be about 50" for a man's tie, or 40" to 45" for a boy's—somewhat longer or shorter, or wider or narrower, according to taste. It is very easy to control the length and width of each section by comparing the knitting, as you go along, to an old tie that can be used as a model. For a single-thickness knitted tie, just stretch out the old tie and lay the knitting on top of it. For a double-thickness knitted tie, open the seam on the back of the old tie and press it flat for convenient comparing.

To begin, cast on 3 stitches. Work 1 wrong-side row. Begin working in any pattern stitch (mosaic patterns are especially nice for neckties), increasing one stitch at each side of the piece every other row for Section 1. Keep the pattern correct, developing additional pattern repeats as new stitches are added. When you can see by comparison with your model that sufficient width has been attained, stop increasing. You are ready to begin Section 2. At this point a single-thickness tie may have about 37 stitches, or a double-thickness tie about 75 stitches, depending, of course, on your stitch gauge and your desired width.

Now begin decreasing 1 stitch at each side of the piece every eighth row, to make the gradual taper of Section 2. If you are making a wide tie with a sharper-than-average taper, you might want to decrease every sixth row; or, if you are making a narrow tie with a very gradual taper, you might want to decrease every tenth row. But decreases every eighth row will be about right for the normal shape. After working 4″ or 5″ of Section 2, check with your model. If the edges of the knitting do not seem to be slanting at the right angle, you can always speed up or slow down the rate of decreasing for a better match.

When the tie is narrow enough for the straight neck portion (Section 3), you are ready to work even throughout this longest section. The width here should not be much more than an inch for a single-thickness tie, or 2 inches for a double-thickness tie. Continue working in pattern on these few stitches until the piece measures about 36″ or 37″ from the beginning. Then begin Section 4, increasing 1 stitch at each side of the piece every eighth row. Section 4 is neither so long nor so wide as Section 2, and may be finished at a width of about 25 stitches for a single-thickness tie or 51 stitches for a double-thickness tie, again depending on your own gauge and desired width. Two-thirds the width of the first, widest point is about right for the second point.

Finally, for Section 5, decrease 1 stitch at each side of the piece every other row until only 3 stitches remain. Knit the last 3 stitches together, draw the yarn end through the last stitch, and finish.

General hints: It is a good idea to *press* the tie as you go along, because pressing will cause it to lengthen somewhat. Therefore the unpressed knitted fabric will appear shorter than it really is. It is also a good idea to start sewing the seam in a double-thickness tie when the knitting is only about half finished. Thread the yarn needle and draw the lower outside corners together at the back of the tie. Weave the seam from the right side, carefully matching corresponding ends of the same rows. Mosaic patterns make this particularly easy to do, because their side edges show alternating stripes of color. Mosaic patterns also give a choice of fabric effects: they may be knitted on wrong-side rows for a nubby garter-stitch type of fabric, or purled on wrong-side rows for a smooth stockinette-stitch type of fabric, or worked in combination with the wrong-side rows of one color knitted, the wrong-side rows of the other color purled.

A double-thickness tie usually requires no lining or interfacing. Neither does a single-thickness tie if the stitches are small and the fabric therefore close-grained and firm. But if you want to add a lining to your single-thick-ness tie, it's easy. Just cut a piece of fabric on the bias, using the tie as a pattern, fold the raw edges under, and stitch it carefully to the back of the tie.

To make neat side edges on a single-thickness tie, where the side edges will be exposed, slip the first stitch of every row, holding the yarn to the wrong side each time. Work increases or decreases just inside the edge stitches, not on the edges themselves.

A tie with straight, horizontal lower ends—instead of points—can be made by omitting Sections 1 and 5. In this case, begin by casting on the number of stitches required for the maximum width and start the gradual decreases of Section 2 right away; at the end of Section 4, just bind off all stitches.

A broad, soft tie for a woman's blouse or suit can be made in the same manner as a man's tie. The proportions are just a little different, and the fabric may be lace or some other openwork pattern. A knitted sash also benefits by the gentle decrease-and-increase shaping demonstrated by a necktie. In the case of a sash, it is usually desirable to have both ends the same width, so the number of decrease rows and increase rows would be equal; and the straight portion, to go around the waist, would of course be longer.

Increased Poncho

(Color 5)

A poncho worked from the neck down, with increases, is the simplest of all shaped garments. Neither its shaping nor its patterns need to be planned in advance. It is strictly an improvisational work, made up as you go along. It can be knitted in rounds on a circular needle, or it can be knitted in rows as two separate halves, or as four separate quarters.

To begin a seamless circular-knit poncho, measure loosely around your neck and multiply this measurement by your stitch gauge, rounding off the total to the nearest number divisible by 4. With a 16" circular needle, cast on this number of stitches. Place 4 markers on the needle to divide

COLOR 1. *Straight-strip wall hanging worked in Shadow 43 with five colors, alternating by Method III (multicolor reversal)*

COLOR 2. *Sampler-square afghan in an assortment of 48 mosaic, band, and shadow patterns*

COLOR 3. *Bias strip wall hanging or stole, worked in Bands 6, 7, 12–15, 25, 35, 39–42, 46, 47, 49, 53–55, 57, 58, 60, 61, 63, 66, 69, and 72*

COLOR 4. *Two mosaic-patterned neckties*

COLOR 5. *Increased poncho worked in Bands 3, 8, 16, 20, 22, 24, 30, 34, and 37, all counterchanged by Method I, with knitted pants featuring Bands 11, 14, 28, and 29*

COLOR 6. *Three sweaters worked in Shadows 9, 29, and 51, each with three colors alternating by Method III (multicolor reversal)*

COLOR 7. *Scrap-yarn coat worked in Shadows 5–7, 10, 13, 14, 19, 25, 27, 35, 37, 38, 45–47, 50–53, 55, 56, 58, and 61–64, with front border of Band 8*

COLOR 9. *Sleeveless blouse worked in Mosaics 10, 12, 37, 47, 56, and 80; Band 5; and Shadows 3 and 39; and a long vest decorated with mosaic patterns in metallic thread*

COLOR 10. *Basic basketweave skirt in six colors*

COLOR 11. *Mosaic-patterned basketweave bag, worked in Band 33 with six colors*

the stitches into 4 equal parts. These markers indicate the center front, center back, and left and right shoulders.

Work your mosaic patterns in rounds, increasing 1 stitch each side of each marker, a total of 8 increases, on every other round. As more stitches are added, you can change to a 24″ needle, then a 29″ needle, then a 36″ needle. During the first needle change, when the growing poncho can be spread over the shoulders as far as the top of each arm (check this by slipping it over your head and spreading it out while there are two needles in it), remove the left and right shoulder markers and stop increasing at those points. Continue center back and center front increases as before, a total of 4 increases, every other round all the way to the lower edge. When it reaches to the wrist on each side, or to the desired length, bind off.

Helpful hint: Toward the bottom, the circular-knit poncho will have many stitches, perhaps too many to fit comfortably on one 36″ needle. You can change to an even longer needle if you have one, or else you can work on 3 or 4 circular needles by passing from one to the next just as you use a set of double-pointed sock needles.

To make the same poncho in two separate halves, begin by casting on half the stitches required to go around the neck. Make sure it is an even number, and place a marker in the exact center, to indicate one shoulder. Increase 1 stitch each side of this center marker and 1 stitch at each side edge, a total of 4 increases, every other row until the shoulder point is reached. Remove the marker and continue the half-poncho by increasing 1 stitch at each side edge, a total of 2 increases, every other row to the desired length. Make the other half the same way. Sew them together along center-front and center-back seams.

To break the poncho down even further into four separate quarters, begin with ¼ of the neck stitches. Increase 1 stitch each side of the piece every other row to the shoulder point, then work one side even while you continue the increases at the other side. For the right front and left back pieces, the shoulder increases will be ended on the right-hand side. For the left front and right back pieces, the shoulder increases will be ended on the left-hand side. Sew all four finished pieces together.

The increased poncho is an ideal project in which to display a series of mosaic bands in various colors and patterns, and it is easily made by the dramatic counterchanging technique that causes any mosaic pattern to sparkle in positive-negative color combinations.

OPPOSITE: *Figure 171. Four mosaic handbags. Upper left: Bands 56, 59, 66, and 71; upper right: Mosaic 59 counterchanged by Method 2; lower left: Shadow 19 variation; lower right: Band 80 with motifs alternating in half-drop formation*

Figure 170. Handbag worked in Shadow 44 with three colors, alternating by Method III, multicolor reversal

Handbags

(Figures 35, 170, 171, 193, and 194)

A mosaic handbag can be made in a variety of ways. The simplest form is the unshaped straight strip—either two rectangles sewed together back to back, or a single strip folded in half and sewed together at the sides. The next simplest form is the unshaped straight tube, worked on a circular

needle and sewed together at the bottom. You can add a little shaping to either of these forms, so the bag will be slightly wider at the bottom than at the top. If such a bag is worked from the top down, the shaping is done with increases; if it is worked from the bottom up, the shaping is done with decreases.

For example, consider a seamless tubular bag worked on a circular needle from the top down. To begin it, decide on a number of inches around the top of the bag, multiply by your stitch gauge, and cast this number of stitches onto a circular needle. Use an even number, so it can be divided into identical halves. On the first round, place 1 marker at the beginning, and a second marker exactly halfway around. These markers indicate the sides of the bag, where the increasing will be done. Work in pattern, increasing 1 stitch each side of each marker every inch or so, until the bag is long enough and wide enough to suit you. While working the last inch at the bottom of the bag, decrease 1 stitch each side of each marker every other round, to cut off the lower corners so they won't stick out too much. Place the remaining stitches on 2 separate needles, 1 for each side. Weave the stitches together, taking them alternately off the needles one by one.

Of course the same shape can be worked in the other direction, from the bottom up. It can also be worked on straight needles in two separate pieces, to be sewed together at the sides and bottom, or in one straight piece, to be folded and sewed together at the sides. The latter can be shaped in two ways: (1) Cast on at the top and make half the bag from the top down, increasing to widen it, then continue the same piece to make the other half of the bag from the bottom up, decreasing to reverse shaping; (2) cast on at the bottom and knit half the bag from the bottom up, decreasing to narrow it; bind off at the top; then pick up stitches from the cast-on edge and knit the other half to match. When working a bag in two separate pieces, increase or decrease one stitch at a time at each side edge.

To make the simplest kind of lining for a bag, fold the lining fabric and lay the finished bag on it with the bottom of the bag along the fold. Mark the outline of sides and top on the fabric, $\frac{1}{2}''$ away from bag edges. Cut the folded fabric through both thicknesses along the outline. Turn top edges of the fabric under to the wrong side in a $\frac{3}{4}''$ hem. With right sides of the fabric together, stitch side seams $\frac{3}{4}''$ in from edges. Sew ends of separate bag handles firmly to the wrong side of the lining, then insert the lining into the bag, wrong side of fabric against wrong side of knitting. Pin and hand-stitch the knitted edge to the lining all around the top. Add a zipper if desired.

To make separate bag handles, you need two cords or straps, between 14″ and 20″ long, according to taste. These can be knitted, crocheted, braided, or simply twisted cords. They can be made of matching yarn, tubular ribbon, tape, string, twine, fishline, or any other material that appeals to you. Here are 3 good ways to knit bag handles:

1. With a pair of short, straight needles, cast on an even number of stitches (about 14–22). * Knit 1 stitch, slip the next stitch with yarn in front; repeat from * across row. Work every row the same way until the length is right. This method makes a narrow seamless tube in stockinette stitch, even though it is worked back and forth in rows—a rather remarkable accomplishment, and interesting for you to try if you've never seen it done before.

2. With a pair of short, straight needles, cast on an odd number of stitches (about 9–19). *Row 1*—K1, * sl 1 with yarn in front, k1; repeat from *. *Row 2*—Sl 1 with yarn in back, * pl, sl 1 with yarn in back; repeat from *. Repeat these 2 rows until the length is right. This method makes a firm, flat band of dense knitting, called fabric stitch, that has very little stretch and so makes a good strap for a handle.

3. With a pair of double-pointed needles, cast on 3 stitches. Knit 3, then slide the stitches to the other end of the same needle, without turning, and again knit 3; repeat the same process throughout, until the length is right. This method (called "Idiot's Delight," for reasons that will become obvious to you when you try it) makes a very narrow tubular cord suitable for any small, lightweight design such as an evening bag.

Place Mats

(Figures 74 and 172)

Mosaic-patterned place mats are delightful accessories for your table. You can work them in bright informal combinations of several colors, or in a more restrained scheme of just two colors to match your dining-room decor.

Each mat in your set can display a different pattern. A table laid with such knitted creations is both unusual and charming.

Naturally, you can knit a place mat as a plain straight-strip rectangle, adding a border around the outside edges. You can also knit it as a seamless rectangle on circular needles, working outward from a central cast-on "slot" to a final continuous bind-off. This method makes a very elegant design. The following explains how to do it.

Choose a suitable material—linen or cotton yarn, crochet cotton, string, metallic thread, a hard-twist synthetic or "straw" yarn (be sure it's washable)—and knit your test swatch, using a garter-stitch fabric. Decide how many stitches you'll need to make a width of about 5". If your chosen pattern is a bisymmetrical one with an obvious central stitch, plan this width with an even multiple plus 1 more stitch. This will enable you to

Figure 172. Set of four mosaic place mats. Upper left: Mosaic 55; upper right: Mosaic 49; lower left: Mosaic 51; lower right: Mosaic 109. Note matched and reversed patterning along corner increase lines

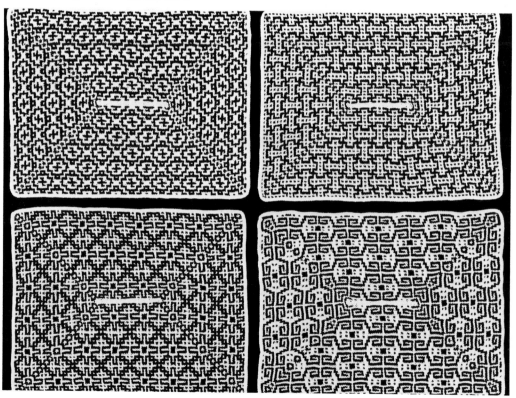

center the pattern so that the motifs will match neatly across the increasing corners as you work (see below).

For the central slot, *double* the number of stitches in the 5″ width. Add 6 stitches more. Loosely cast on this total, using a 16″ circular needle or a set of sock needles, and join. Purl 1 round, marking the stitches in the following sequence: 1 corner stitch, 1 stitch to begin the first short side of the rectangle, a second corner stitch, 5″ of stitches to begin the first long side of the rectangle, a third corner stitch, 1 stitch to begin the second short side, a fourth corner stitch, and 5″ of stitches to begin the second long side. Join the second color and begin your pattern. On every other round—that is, on the second round of each color—make a double increase in each of the 4 corner stitches (or a single increase on each side of each corner stitch) so 8 new stitches are added on each increase round. Develop the pattern, according to its chart, as new stitches are added to each of the 4 sections.

Matching a bisymmetrical pattern across the increasing corners is a refinement of design, very necessary in an article like a place mat, which ought to be a little gem of knitting artistry. You wouldn't want your mats to look sloppy, confused, or incompetently executed, with distortions of pattern lines in the shaping. Therefore you should always center such a pattern on each long side of the rectangle as you knit the first pattern round, by using a correct multiple plus 1 stitch. The single stitch that begins each short side is also a pattern center. Every new stitch on one side of an increasing corner is worked the same as the corresponding stitch on the other side of the same corner. Once you've arranged your pattern symmetrically on the first round, it will develop evenly along each corner on all subsequent increase rounds. You won't have to think about it again, because the matching takes place automatically as you increase. But do think about it at the start, and plan the stitch count for centered patterns whenever you can. Study the diagonal corners of the mats shown in the picture, and you'll see how important such a designing detail can be.

As your stitches increase, you can switch to a 24″ needle, later to a 29″ needle, and still later to a 36″ needle if you wish. Keep working until your place mat is about 13″ by 18″, or the desired size. Bind off all the way around. Weave together the cast-on stitches of the central slot.

The same one-piece design can be worked back and forth in rows if you prefer. Figure the total number of cast-on stitches as for the seamless version, then add 1 more stitch. On the first row, mark the stitches as follows: 1 edge (corner) stitch, 1 stitch for the first short side, a second corner stitch, 5" of stitches, a third corner stitch, 1 stitch for the second short side, a fourth corner stitch, 5" of stitches, and a final edge (corner) stitch. Work the same as a seamless mat but make the open-edge increases, each end of every other row, single instead of double. When the mat is finished, sew the open corner together in a diagonal seam.

Increased place mats are very effective when worked in bands of different patterns, as well as in a single all-over pattern. Try them both ways. After you have a complete set for your own table, you can go on making new sets for the ideal Christmas, birthday, shower, or wedding gift. They will always be welcome and useful.

Banded Skirt

(Figures 76, 173, 174, 175, and 183)

A skirt worked from the waist down is very easy to knit in a series of mosaic-patterned bands. The shaping is simple, flexible, and readily planned one step at a time. Each band is worked on its own multiple of stitches, the total number of stitches remaining the same until the pattern for that band is completed. Between bands, there are increase rounds (or rows) to make the skirt grow in width.

To begin a seamless skirt, take a 24" circular needle, cast on as many stitches as you need to go around your waist, join, and work a waistband. Choose your first mosaic band pattern. On the next round, *increase* as many stitches, evenly spaced around the skirt, as you need to make an even multiple of that pattern—without edge stitches. For example, suppose your waistband has 120 stitches. Just below the waist, you'd like to have at least 124 stitches. The pattern you want to use first has a multiple of 14. $9 \times 14 = 126$, so you can increase 6 stitches to make an even multiple. 120 divided by 6 is 20, so you can space the increases evenly in this round by increasing in every twentieth stitch.

After the first band is finished, measure the *length* of the knitting so far, then measure yourself (loosely) that many inches below the waist. Multiply by your stitch gauge to find out how many stitches are needed to go around you in an easy fit at that level. (Never skimp on stitches; a skirt should not be tight.) Choose your second mosaic band pattern. Let's say this one has a multiple of 12, and your total stitch requirement here is at least 138. 11 × 12 = 132, which is not quite wide enough; so you add one more repeat to make it 12 × 12 = 144. To achieve this number, you need 18 new stitches. 126 divided by 18 is 7, so you can space the increases evenly in this round by increasing in every seventh stitch.

After the second band is finished, again measure the length of the knitting, then measure yourself that far below the waist. Multiply by your stitch gauge. Perhaps you need a width of at least 156 stitches now, and the pattern you've chosen for your third band has a multiple of 16. 10 × 16 = 160, the nearest higher number for an even multiple. To make this total you'll need to add 16 new stitches. 144 divided by 16 is 9, so you can space the increases evenly in this round by increasing in every ninth stitch.

Here is all the figuring done so far, in condensed form:

Waistband—no. of sts required, 120.

Pattern band 1—no. of sts required, at least 124. Pattern multiple, 14. 9 × 14 = 126. No. of sts to be added to 120: 6. 120 divided by 6 = 20. Increase in every twentieth st.

Pattern band 2—no. of sts required, at least 138. Pattern multiple, 12. 12 × 12 = 144. No. of sts to be added to 126: 18. 126 divided by 18 = 7. Increase in every seventh st.

Pattern band 3—no. of sts required, at least 156. Pattern multiple, 16. 10 × 16 = 160. No. of sts to be added to 144: 16. 144 divided by 16 = 9. Increase in every ninth st.

Figure all subsequent bands in the same way, going from one level to the next until your skirt is long enough. To check the length, you can try on the seamless skirt any time, while changing from a shorter circular needle to a longer one as the stitches multiply. With some of the stitches on one needle and some on the other, the skirt can be spread out for trying on, and even pressed as you go along. When the desired length is reached,

Figure 173. Seamless banded skirt in an assortment of mosaic and band patterns

Figure 174. Seamless banded skirt in three colors with Shadows 21 and 35 alternating by Method III, Shadows 16 and 62 alternating by Method IV

Figure 175. Seamless banded skirt in Bands 2, 6, 8, and 12; and Shadows 28, 41, 46, 50, 51, 53, and 57, each worked twice by Method V

work a few rounds in plain garter stitch or some other noncurling pattern, and bind off.

Helpful hint: It's best to place increase rounds closer together at the top of the skirt, and farther apart at the bottom, because you need to increase width faster in the hip area. Therefore, put narrower pattern bands near the waist and wider ones lower down on the skirt.

If you prefer to knit back and forth in rows, instead of working in rounds on a circular needle, you can construct the same kind of skirt in one piece and sew the side edges together in a single seam. Or, you can make the same skirt in separate halves, thirds, or quarters, and put it together with two, three, or four seams. No matter how many pieces you want to make of it, each piece is worked on the appropriate fraction of the total stitch requirement to suit the measurement at any level. Add 1 extra edge stitch on each side of each separate piece. These edge stitches will disappear into the seams when the skirt is sewed together. Inside the edge stitches, plan each pattern so that it will match across the seam for a neat, finished, professional look.

Your tape measure and your test swatch are the simple, basic starting points for an elegantly banded skirt of any size, length, and fullness. Once you have tried and comprehended this method of making a skirt, you'll find it so much more satisfactory than the usual commercial methods that you'll probably never need or want to use a commercial skirt pattern again.

Counterchanged Designs

(Color 5, Figures 176, 177, 178, 179, 180, 181, 182, and 183)

Since any mosaic pattern can be worked in both positive (dark-on-light) and negative (light-on-dark) versions, it's possible to create many interesting design effects by combining both versions in the same garment or other project. Of course a simple way to do this is to alternate the two versions in contrasting horizontal bands. And every shadow mosaic provides an example of positive-negative patterning carried out through a series of horizontal rows.

There are also several easy methods for *vertically* dividing positive and negative versions of a mosaic pattern. I call this process counterchanging, because it substitutes the dark color for the light color, or vice versa, across the vertical line. It is particularly attractive in garments that are quartered by such vertical lines, so that different versions of the pattern appear in the left-front, right-front, left-back, and right-back quarters. The following descriptions of counterchanging methods are based on this design idea, where patterns are changed at the center-back and center-front lines of a garment. But bear in mind that you can also use vertical counterchanging in many other arrangements and in many different kinds of knitted articles.

Counterchanging Method 1, joining separate pieces—The simplest (though crudest) way to counterchange a pattern is to work each portion of the item separately, and sew center lines together. For example, you might make the right half of a garment back in a positive version of the pattern, such as black on white; then make the left half in a negative version of the same pattern, white on black, using black yarn to represent the white squares on the chart and white yarn to represent the black squares. Make the garment front similarly divided in two pieces, and sew the four quarters together at center and side seams, carefully matching pattern rows. To use up odds and ends of leftover yarn, you could even work an entirely different color combination in each quarter, so the finished garment would display eight colors altogether in its counterchanged quarters. Remember that, when pattern rows are matched along a center or a side edge in this way, you should always try to balance the motifs symmetrically on both sides. This is easily done, without stitch-counting, by working the right-hand piece first, then beginning each right-side row of the left-hand piece at the point where the previous corresponding row ended, and working in the reverse direction (see "Bias Strips and Squares").

Counterchanging Method 2, alternating one color in the same piece—In this method you work the full front or back of the garment at once, without a center seam. Use Color A for foundation row(s). Join Color B. Work pattern Row 1 with B as far as the center line. Join Color C. Drop B strand at the center and finish the same row across the left half with C. Work pattern Row 2 on the wrong side with C, back to the center line. Drop C strand at the center, pick up B, and finish the other half of the same wrong-side row with B. Then with A, work pattern Rows 3 and 4 all the way across. With B, work Row 5 to the center line, drop B and finish the same row with C. With C, work Row 6 to the center line, drop C and finish the same row with B. Then with A, work Rows 7 and 8 all the way across as before. Continue in the same manner, changing colors at the center on each B–C row, always dropping these strands on the wrong side of the work and picking up each second strand from under the first one so that no holes will be left. The same pattern thus appears in A and B on the right half of the piece, and in A and C on the left half.

Counterchanging Method 3, alternating both colors in the same piece—Here the result is the same as in Method 1, but the piece is worked full width, without a seam in the center. Use 4 strands of yarn, 2 of each color. Work the first right-side foundation row with A to the center line. Join Color B. Drop A and finish the same row with B. Work the next wrong-side foundation row with B to the center line. Drop B and finish the same row with A. Join the second B strand at the right-hand edge. With B, work Pattern Row 1 to the center line. Join the second A strand. Drop B and finish the same row with A. Work Row 2 with the same A strand on the wrong side back to the center. Drop A and finish the same row with B. Work Row 3 with A to the center. Drop A and finish the same row with B. Work Row 4 with B to the center. Drop B and finish the same row with A. Continue as in these 4 rows, always changing colors at the center line. This method produces a true counterchange, as both colors reverse on every row. With 4 strands in use, there is always an extra strand of the proper color waiting at the center line, and another extra strand waiting at the right-hand edge, so each row can pass smoothly from the positive to the negative version of the pattern.

Counterchanging Method 4, alternating pattern rows with the same color—For this method, only 2 strands are needed. The positive-negative contrast is achieved by allowing the pattern to lag 2 rows behind itself on one half of the piece. Work foundation row(s) with A, placing a marker on the needle at the center line. Join B. With B, work Pattern Row 1 to the marker. After slipping the marker, jump up 1 line on the chart and work Pattern Row 3 to the end. On the wrong side, return with B to the right-hand edge in the usual way. Then with A, work Pattern

Row 3 to the marker. Jump up 1 more line on the chart and work Pattern Row 5 to the end, returning on the wrong side as usual. On the next right-side row, work Row 5 to the marker, then Row 7 to the end. Continue in this same way throughout, so that the left half of the piece produces the negative version of the pattern automatically by anticipating the design, always 2 rows ahead of the right half. This method is ideal for making seamless garments in circular knitting, where an extra strand or two at each vertical counterchange line would result in a tangle of too many strands. To quarter a seamless garment, just place markers on the circular needle at side and center points, and change row numbers at these points as you work around. You can also create a seamless garment with 6 or 8 counterchange lines, if you wish, for you can use any number of markers on a circular needle and change row numbers at as many different places as you like. A seamless skirt, for example, is very effective when vertically striped with pattern counterchanges in this manner. In this case, be sure to increase evenly in each segment on each increase round, so the stripes will broaden at the same rate as they grow toward the bottom of the skirt.

Figure 176. Horizontally counterchanged seamless sweater worked in Mosaics 8, 37, 41, and 51; Bands 29 and 31, each pattern repeated in reverse for positive-negative contrast

Figure 177. Vertically counterchanged straight-strip wall hanging in Mosaics 10, 39, 44, 49, 57, 87, 104, and 109; Bands 28, 30, and 38, with a counterchanged border of Band 12, all alternating by Method 3. Note matched and reversed patterning at corner increase lines

Figure 178. Seamless counterchanged sweater in Mosaic 100, alternated by Method 4. Note that motifs on left front lag two pattern rounds behind motifs on right front

Figure 179. Seamless counterchanged jacket in Mosaic 53, alternated by Method 4

Figure 180. Seamless counter-changed jacket, back detail, showing lines of pattern lag at sides and center back

OPPOSITE: *Figure 181. Counterchanged coat in Shadows 6, 9, 16, 17, 21, 22, 26, 27, 34, 47, 48, and 57, all alternating by Method II, pattern reversal*

BELOW: *Figure 182. Counterchanged coat, back detail, showing counterchanging Method I at side seams, Method II at center back*

Mosaic-Patterned Garments

(Colors 6, 7, 8, and 9; Figures 184, 185, 186, 187, 188, 189, 190, 191, 192, 193, 194, and 195)

Mosaic patterns can be used, either sparingly or lavishly, in a garment of any size, shape, and style. Illustrations in this book show a few examples, to give you some basic ideas. You can apply these ideas, and many others, to your own knitting, to create your own original fashions.

If, for a particular garment, you choose to follow commercial pattern directions, you can easily apply those directions to mosaic knitting. Just be sure that your mosaic test swatch works to the same gauge that the directions call for. If the garment is worked in plain stockinette stitch, you'll find that the mosaic-knit fabric usually tends to be a bit tighter. With the recommended needle size, therefore, you may need more stitches to achieve any particular width; so you may want to follow the directions for a size larger than the one you want. Alternatively, you can use larger needles to achieve the required stitch gauge for your own size.

Of course a more satisfactory way to knit garments is to work from your own measurements with your own gauge, instead of following commercial directions, which may or may not produce a perfect fit. Methods for taking your own measurements, and working any garment style to fit them, are given in another one of my books, *Knitting from the Top*. All the garments shown in this book have been designed according to directions given in that one.

Try mosaic patterns in your own sweaters, coats, dresses, skirts, pants, and other garments, using them as all-over fabric designs, as borders, or as trim. Baby clothes and children's garments are perky and colorful when decorated with mosaic patterns. Almost anything you knit can be brightened up, and made more excitingly original, with the use of mosaic patterning.

Figure 183. Seamless ten-gore skirt worked in counterchanged panels of Mosaics 43, 73, 83, 103, 109, and 110, all alternating by Method IV. Note that each pattern is placed two rounds lower (that is, later) on light-colored panels than on dark-colored ones

Figure 184. Shadow 4 worked by Method II as decorative trim on a seamless two-piece dress

Figure 185. Band 38 and Shadows 29, 35, and 40 as decorative trim on a tunic-and-pants set

Figure 186. Sleeveless V-neck pullover worked in Mosaic 91 with borders of Band 86

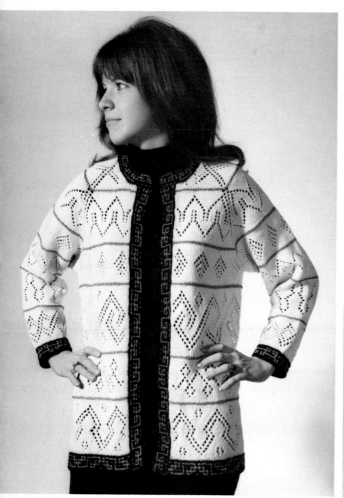

Figure 187. Bands 3, 6, 11, and 12 as decorative borders on a lace-patterned jacket

Figure 188. Seamless pullover worked in Shadow 60 with three colors alternating by Method III

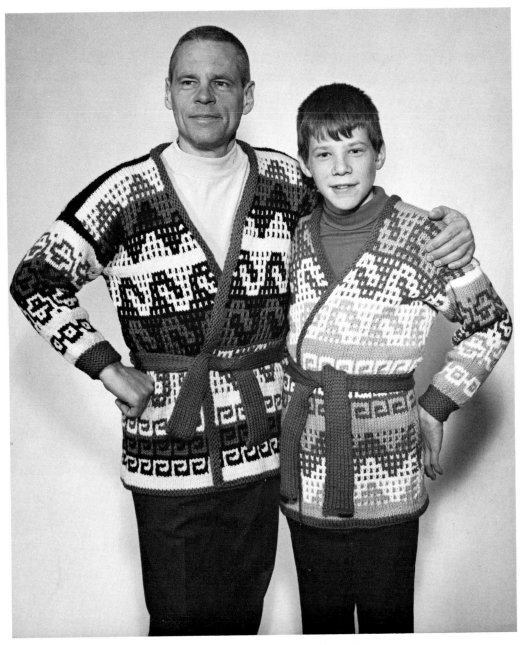

Figure 189. Wraparound jackets in Shadows 16, 32, and 40, in three colors alternating by Method III

Figure 190. Seamless one-piece dress in Mosaics 13, 40, 44, 48, 51, 80, 84, and 109; Bands 34, 35, and 39; and Shadow 4. Note matched and reversed patterning at center front. Increases for flared skirt are worked between pattern bands as for seamless banded skirt

Figure 191. V-neck cardigan in Shadows 17, 20, 21, 25, 53, and 61, each with three colors alternating by Method III

Figure 192. Seamless two-piece suit in an assortment of mosaic and band patterns. For complete skirt, see Figure 173

Figure 193. Seamless two-piece suit with jacket worked in Shadows 29, 30, 32, 40, and 41 alternating by Method III; Shadows 4, 9, and 14 alternating by Method IV. For complete skirt, see Figure 174; matching bag, Figure 170

Figure 194. Seamless two-piece suit with jacket worked in Bands 3, 5, and 9; Shadows 2, 3, 11, 14, 16, 18, 21–23, 28, 29, 47, 55, and 60, each worked twice by Method V. For complete skirt, see Figure 175; matching bag, Figure 35

Figure 195. Seamless jacket in Bands 50, 51, 53, 62, 67, 74, 75, and 78, with borders of Band 9

5

BASKETWEAVE KNITTING

Basketweave knitting is an easy and fascinating technique used to make articles that seem to be worked in diagonally woven strips. This appearance is an illusion. Actually, basketweave knitting is not diagonally woven strips, but a seamless construction of separate diagonal segments worked one at a time. With basketweave knitting you can create tubular articles, such as bags, skirts, and pillow covers, without seams even though all the knitting goes back and forth in rows.

Articles made with this technique require no finishing, pressing, or blocking. The tendency of stockinette stitch (plain knitting) to curl at the edges—which is nothing but a nuisance in other kinds of shaping—is used to great advantage in basketweave knitting, and helps to create the illusion of interwoven strands.

The technique involves only a very few basic knitting operations. All you have to know is (1) how to knit, (2) how to purl, (3) how to purl 2 stitches together, (4) how to knit 2 stitches together through the back loops, (5) how to turn short rows, and (6) how to pick up stitches both knitwise and purlwise.

The first 4 of these operations are well known to every knitter. The last 2 are known to nearly every knitter, and will be described in detail for those who may be unsure about them. Even beginners can master basketweave knitting quickly, and learn to create some really fascinating designs, the appearance of which may mystify an expert.

Basic Basketweave Method

To start a seamless-tube design in basketweave knitting, take a circular needle, cast on stitches, and join them in the usual way. The number of stitches you cast on will depend on two questions: (1) how many segments will there be, and (2) how many stitches per segment? These numbers can be anything, to suit any width. You might have 10 segments of 10 stitches each (100 stitches), or 12 segments of 6 stitches each (72 stitches), or 19 segments of 5 stitches each (95 stitches), or 15 segments of 8 stitches each (120 stitches), or any other combination. The only rule is that no matter how many segments there are, every one should have the same number of stitches.

After casting on, knit a foundation round of triangular half-segments shaped by short rows. This foundation round is worked only once. Its purpose is to establish the diagonal angle that will be used throughout the rest of the knitting.

Foundation round—Work each segment as follows: * k2, turn, p2, turn, k3, turn, p3, turn, k4, turn, p4, turn, and continue in this manner, taking 1 more stitch before each right-side turn, until you have worked as many stitches as you want the segment to have. After making the last right-side turn and purling back to the right-hand edge (which is raising itself above the needle in a triangular shape), knit once more across this first segment and begin again from * to work the second segment in the same way. When all segments, all the way around the needle, have been worked like this, the foundation round is finished.

Turn the short rows this way: Knit to the turning point, bring the yarn forward between the needles, slip the next stitch with yarn in front, put the yarn to the back again, and return the slip-stitch to the left needle point. Turn the work around to the wrong side and purl. This method of passing the yarn around an unworked stitch will prevent holes in the knitting.

There are only 2 pattern rounds in basketweave knitting. Now you are ready to work the first of them. Break the yarn and rejoin it at the upper point of the first triangular segment in the foundation round. If you want to do your basketweave knitting in two colors, introduce the second color here instead of rejoining the same color again.

First pattern round—With wrong side facing, pick up *purlwise* a new set of segment stitches from the side edge of the first segment in the foundation round. When the last of these stitches is picked up, slip it to the left needle point and purl it together with the first stitch of the following segment in the foundation round. * Turn to the right side and knit across. Turn, purl to the last stitch, purl this last stitch together with the next stitch of the following segment. Repeat from * until all stitches of the following segment have been used. After purling the last of these stitches into the new segment, keep the wrong side facing and again pick up *purlwise* a new set of segment stitches from the side edge of the next segment in the foundation round. Continue in the same manner, building a new segment upon each exposed side edge, all the way around.

This first pattern round contains the only operation that may be really unfamiliar: picking up stitches purlwise, from the wrong side. Most knitters are used to picking up stitches from the right side, as if knitting without a left-hand needle. Just as a purl stitch is a knit stitch in reverse, so picking up stitches purlwise is the reverse of picking them up knitwise. Holding the yarn in front, in purl position, insert the needle from behind under the 2 outermost strands of the side edge, wrap the yarn around the needle point as for a purl stitch, and back the needle out to the right side just like ordinary purling. If you've never done this before, it may seem awkward at first, just as plain purling seems awkward when you begin to learn it after plain knitting. But with a little practice you will soon be able to "purl up" stitches from the wrong side as easily as you "knit up" stitches from the right side.

When the first pattern round is finished, break the yarn and rejoin it at the upper point of the last segment made—or, if you are using two colors, rejoin the first color again. Now you are ready to work the other pattern round.

Second pattern round—With right side facing, pick up knitwise—that is, in the usual way—a new set of segment stitches from the side edge of the first segment of the preceding round. When the last of these stitches is picked up, slip it to the left needle point and knit it together through *back* loops with the first stitch of the following segment. * Turn to the wrong side and purl across. Turn, knit to the last stitch, knit this last stitch together through back loops with the next stitch of the following segment. Repeat from * until all stitches of the following segment have been used. After knitting the last of these stitches into the new segment, keep the right side facing and again pick up knitwise a new set of segment stitches from the side edge of the next segment in the preceding round. Continue in the same manner, building a new segment upon each exposed side edge, all the way around.

Of course, in the second pattern round, you are picking up stitches in the usual way, holding the yarn behind the work and drawing it through the side edge as if you were knitting.

At the end of this round, break the yarn and rejoin it at the outer point of the first segment, to start again with the first pattern round. Change colors again, here, if you are using 2 different ones. Repeat the two pattern rounds to the desired length.

General Hints for Basic Basketweave Knitting

In practice you will discover that each segment in basketweave knitting is almost twice as many rows long as the number of stitches picked up for it, less 1 row. Therefore the smoothest join between segments can be achieved by picking up 1 stitch from every other row, with the first and last stitches picked up from the first and last pair of strands in the corners. It's important to pick up stitches right into the corners, otherwise there might be holes left in the work where 4 segments come together. Pick up the first stitch right under the needle; then pick up a stitch from every other row down to the other corner; pick up the last stitch right next to the corner by inserting the needle under the last 2 edge strands of the preceding segment.

If you'd rather not have to turn the work around so often, you can teach yourself to knit from left to right as well as from right to left. Then you can work each segment on the right side only, going back and forth without ever having to turn to the wrong side. Ordinarily, knitting from left to right is just a stunt, without much practical value. But in basketweave knitting it can be a timesaver.

To do it, insert the left needle point into each stitch from front to back, as if you were going to slip the stitch from the right needle. Wrap the yarn *over* (not under) the left needle point and draw it through, thus putting a new stitch on the left needle. When you try this, be sure that the new stitches are standing properly on the left needle, with the right-hand sides of their loops toward you, and are not turned about or twisted. If the stitches line up on the left needle with their left-hand sides toward you, then you are wrapping the yarn incorrectly.

You can knit from left to right either American style or Continental style, holding the yarn with either hand. Like any other new way of knitting, it takes practice. If you are sufficiently interested in learning to knit this way, then you will practice long enough to overcome the initial awkwardness. If you don't want to bother, then you can go on turning your segments to the wrong side in the usual way.

Finishing Basic Basketweave Knitting with a Straight Edge

To end a basketweave article with a straight edge, as it began, you work a final round of triangular half-segments shaped by short rows, like a foundation round in reverse. Let's assume that you have ended with the first pattern round, and now want to make a straight-edge finishing round out of the second. Your segments have 10 stitches each. So, with right side facing, * pick up 10 stitches knitwise from the side edge of the first segment of the preceding round. When the tenth stitch has been picked up, slip it to the left needle point and knit it together through back loops with the first stitch of the following segment. Turn, p9, turn, k8, k2 tog-b, turn, p8, turn, k7, k2 tog-b, turn, p7, turn, k6, k2 tog-b, turn, p6, turn, k5, k2 tog-b, turn, p5, turn, k4, k2 tog-b, turn, p4, turn, k3, k2 tog-b, turn, p3, turn, k2, k2 tog-b, turn, p2, turn, k1, k2 tog-b, turn, p1, turn, k2 tog-b. Repeat from * on each segment, all the way around. This leaves all the stitches free on the needle for a final border worked in plain rounds. If you prefer to bind off instead of working a final border, you can simply bind off 1 stitch at a time, at the beginning of each right-side row, instead of turning short rows.

To convert the first pattern round into a straight-edge finishing round, do it the same way as the second pattern round, reversing shaping. This means that you simply turn the short rows 1 stitch farther in on the knit rows each time. So you can finish your basketweave article at any time, whenever it has reached the size that you want.

Basic Basketweave Pillow in Two Colors

(Figure 196)

A little rectangular pillow cover in two cheerful colors is a nice project to begin practicing basketweave knitting. The sample is made with sport yarn in Colors A and B on a 24″ circular needle size 5. There are 10 segments of 10 stitches each—100 cast on.

With A, cast on 100 stitches. Join, being careful not to twist stitches.

Foundation round— * K2, turn, p2, turn, k3, turn, p3, turn, k4, turn, p4, turn, k5, turn, p5, turn, k6, turn, p6, turn, k7, turn, p7, turn, k8, turn, p8, turn, k9, turn, p9, turn, k10, turn, p10, turn, k10; rep from * 9 times more. Break Color A.

First pattern round—Join Color B at upper right corner of first segment made on preceding round. * With wrong side facing, pick up 10 stitches purlwise down side edge of this segment. Put tenth stitch on left needle and purl tog with first stitch of following segment. ** Turn, k10, turn, p9, p2 tog. ** Repeat from ** to ** until all stitches of following segment have been used. Repeat entire sequence from * 9 times more. Break Color B.

Second pattern round—Join Color A at upper left corner of first segment made on preceding round. * With right side facing, pick up 10 stitches knitwise down side edge of this segment. Put tenth stitch on left needle and knit tog-b with first stitch of following segment. ** Turn, p10, turn, k9, k2 tog-b. ** Repeat from ** to ** until all stitches of following segment have been used. Repeat entire sequence from * 9 times more. Break Color A.

Repeat the first and second pattern rounds until the tube is long enough, then work a finishing round to make a straight edge (see preceding description). Work a few rounds of plain garter stitch for final border. Bind off. Make a fabric lining to fit, insert lining into the tube, add stuffing, and sew a zipper under bound-off edges. Attach tassels to corners if desired. Weave cast-on edge together.

Figure 196. Basic basketweave pillow in two colors

Basic Basketweave Bag in Two Colors

(Figure 197)

This sample bag is made exactly like the pillow, with silver and gold metallic yarn on a 24″ circular needle size 3. It has 14 segments of 11 stitches each, 154 stitches cast on. The top is finished with 6 rounds of plain garter stitch. Handles are made of plain stockinette-stitch tubes encasing 14″ lengths of heavy twill tape; ends of handles are sewed to wrong side of lining fabric. Such a bag may be used with or without a zipper closing.

Figure 197. Basic basketweave bag in two colors

Basic Basketweave Skirt in Six Colors:

A DEMONSTRATION OF A SEAMLESS TUBE WITH INCREASE SHAPING

(Color 10)

This sample skirt is worked with lightweight knitting worsted on a size 5 circular needle, and is knitted from the top down. For a 24" waist, it begins with 126 stitches, 18 segments of 7 stitches each. For a larger size, you can (1) use a larger needle, (2) begin with wider segments, or (3) begin with more segments. To use six colors, A, B, C, D, E, and F, alternating them three at a time as in the sample design, you should establish a number of segments divisible by 3 so the color "strips" will be continuous.

With a 24" needle and Color A, then, cast on the required number of stitches, join, and work a waistband in straight garter stitch, ribbing, or any other noncurling pattern. After this, work the foundation round as follows: the first segment in Color A, the second in Color B, the third in Color C, the fourth in A, the fifth in B, the sixth in C, and so on, alternating the first 3 colors. Then work the first pattern round as follows: the first segment in Color D, the second in Color E, the third in Color F, the fourth in D, the fifth in E, the sixth in F, and so on, alternating the last 3 colors. For subsequent pattern rounds, always pick up stitches from any segment with the same color that appears on the *other* side of the segment. This creates an appearance of continuous strips interwoven in a very interesting and colorful fashion.

A skirt must become larger as it grows downward from the waist, so it is shaped with increases. In basketweave knitting, increasing is simplicity itself. For an increase round, just pick up 1 more stitch for each new segment than the preceding segments have. If you have been working segments of 7 stitches, pick up 8 stitches for each segment of the increase round, and continue to work segments of 8 stitches until it is time to increase again to segments of 9 stitches, etc. The row-wise proportions take care of themselves, for each additional stitch means an additional 2 rows on the next pattern round automatically.

Decreases in basketweave knitting, as for a skirt worked from the bottom up, are just as simple; you pick up 1 less stitch for each new segment than the preceding segments have. Increases or decreases are equally invisible; the "woven" strips gradually enlarge or diminish without giving any outward indication of the method by which they are shaped. Such invisible in-pattern shaping is, of course, one of the unique achievements of the craft of knitting, which cannot be duplicated by any other method of garment construction.

The sample skirt is increased to segments of 8 stitches in the second pattern round, and increased again in every third round thereafter. Each increase round naturally adds to the total the same number of new stitches as there are segments. Longer needles may be used as the skirt grows wider, to accommodate the greater numbers of stitches.

When you change colors in every segment, as here, there are many loose yarn ends left hanging on the wrong side of the work. It's a good idea to weave these loose ends into the wrong side as you go, 1 round at a time. Thread each strand into the back of a segment of the same color.

To finish the bottom of a skirt with scallops instead of a straight edge, simply work the final pattern round as usual, using a flat, noncurling fabric such as garter stitch, seed stitch, or moss stitch. Slip the outside edge stitch on every other row. On the last row of each segment, bind off the stitches, then go on to work the next segment in the same way.

Mosaic-Patterned Basketweave Bag

(Color 11)

Now that you know basic basketweave knitting, you can make it even more interesting by adding mosaic patterns to your basketweave projects. As an example, here is a basketweave bag embellished with a simple mosaic pattern on a stockinette-stitch fabric. In working this bag according to the following detailed directions, you will learn how to use any mosaic patterns of your choice in other basketweave designs.

Pattern multiples naturally determine the size of the segments in such a design. In this case, the chosen pattern has a multiple of 16 stitches plus 3 edge stitches. Therefore, single units of the pattern can be conveniently shown on segments of 19 stitches each. The bag has 10 segments, or a total of 190 stitches to be cast on. With Color A, cast on the required total, join, and knit 1 round. To work the foundation round of triangular segments, divide the pattern in half diagonally from the lower right corner to the upper left corner, beginning 2 stitches in from the right-side edge. Look at the "Basketweave Foundation Chart," which shows the original pattern chart so divided. Follow this chart as you work through the written directions row by row. Remember that each row on the chart represents 2 pattern rows of the foundation segment, starting on the right side, with slip-stitches slipped with yarn in back, and then returning on the wrong side, with slip-stitches slipped with yarn in front.

Row 1—With A, k2, turn, p2, turn. (Join Color B.)
Row 2—With B, k1, sl 1, k1, turn, p1, sl 1, p1, turn.
Row 3—With A, k4, turn, p4, turn.
Row 4—With B, (k1, sl 1) twice, k1, turn, p1, (sl 1, p1) twice, turn.
Row 5—With A, k6, turn, p6, turn.
Row 6—With B, (k1, sl 1) twice, k3, turn, p3, (sl 1, p1) twice, turn.
Row 7—With A, k4, (sl 1, k1) twice, turn, (p1, sl 1) twice, p4, turn.
Row 8—With B, k1, sl 1, k5, sl 1, k1, turn, p1, sl 1, p5, sl 1, p1, turn.

Row 9—With A, k2, sl 1, k1, sl 1, k3, sl 1, k1, turn, p1, sl 1, p3, sl 1, p1, sl 1, p2, turn.

Row 10—With B, k1, sl 1, k5, sl 1, k3, turn, p3, sl 1, p5, sl 1, p1, turn.

Row 11—With A, k4, sl 1, k1, sl 1, k5, turn, p5, sl 1, p1, sl 1, p4, turn.

Row 12—With B, (k1, sl 1) twice, k5, sl 1, k3, turn, p3, sl 1, p5, (sl 1, p1) twice, turn.

Row 13—With A, k6, (sl 1, k1) 4 times, turn, (p1, sl 1) 4 times, p6, turn.

Row 14—With B, (k1, sl 1) 3 times, k7, sl 1, k1, turn, p1, sl 1, p7, (sl 1, p1) 3 times, turn.

Row 15—With A, k8, sl 1, k1, sl 1, k5, turn, p5, sl 1, p1, sl 1, p8, turn.

Row 16—With B, (k1, sl 1) 4 times, k3, (sl 1, k1) 3 times, turn, (p1, sl 1) 3 times, p3, (sl 1, p1) 4 times, turn. (Break Color B.)

Row 17—With A, k18, turn, p18, turn.

Row 18—With A, k19. Begin next segment from Row 1.

On the second segment of the foundation round, you can join a different Color B. If you have an even number of segments, you can use

BASKETWEAVE FOUNDATION CHART

White squares = Color A   Black squares = Color B

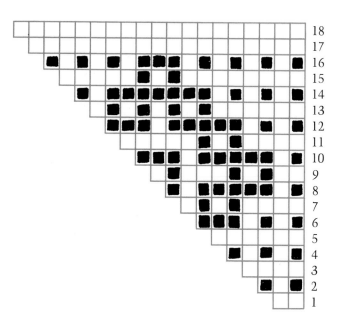

2 different Color B's alternately; or, if you have a number of segments divisible by 3, you can use 3 different Color B's, and so on. The bag shown as an example has 6 colors, 2 different A's and 4 different B's. B colors are used in alternate segments, and A colors are used in alternate rounds.

When the foundation round is finished, join either the same or another Color A for the first pattern round, attaching it to the upper corner of the first segment made. Now you can work from the original pattern chart, making a full unit of the pattern, 19 stitches wide, on each segment. Since the stitches for this round are picked up from the wrong side, the pattern is worked on each segment with wrong-side rows first; so the colors are changed at the left-hand edge of each segment instead of at the right-hand edge as usual. Any mosaic pattern is worked with 2 rows at a time of each color, so it makes no difference whether each color is used on a right-side row followed by a wrong-side row, or a wrong-side row followed by a right-side row. It looks the same either way. To begin with the wrong-side rows you can simply read the lines on the chart from left to right.

First pattern round: * With wrong side facing, pick up 19 stitches purlwise down side edge of preceding segment. When the nineteenth stitch has been picked up, place it on left needle point and purl it together with the first stitch of following segment. Turn, k19, turn, p18, p2 tog, turn, k19. Join Color B and begin the pattern with a wrong-side row. At the end of each wrong-side row, purl the last stitch together with a stitch of the following segment. After the last Color B rows, break Color B. With A, p18, p2 tog, turn, k19, turn, p18, p2 tog. Repeat from * on each segment of this round.

When the first pattern round is finished, join either the same or another Color A for the second pattern round, attaching it to the upper left corner of the first segment made on the first round. * With right side facing, pick up 19 stitches knitwise down the side edge of the segment. When the nineteenth stitch has been picked up, place it on left needle point and knit it together through back loops with the first stitch of following segment. Turn, p19, turn, k18, k2 tog-b, turn, p19. Join Color B and begin the pattern with a right-side row. At the end of each right-side row, knit the last stitch together with a stitch of the following segment through back loops. After the last Color B rows, break Color B. With A, k18, k2 tog-b, turn, p19, turn, k18, k2 tog-b. Repeat from * on each segment of this round.

Continue alternating first and second pattern rounds, changing colors as desired, until the bag is as long as you'd like. For a finishing round, divide the pattern chart diagonally as for the foundation round. If you finish with the second pattern round, the diagonal runs upward from right to left across the chart, and you work the lower left half of the pattern. If you finish with the first pattern round, the diagonal runs upward from left to right across the chart, and you work the lower right half of the pattern. The latter arrangement is shown here to give you the idea (see "Basketweave Finishing Chart"). After the finishing round, decrease about 1 stitch in every 8 or 10 stitches all the way around, to tighten the border, and work a half-inch or so in plain garter stitch to make a neat edge.

BASKETWEAVE FINISHING CHART

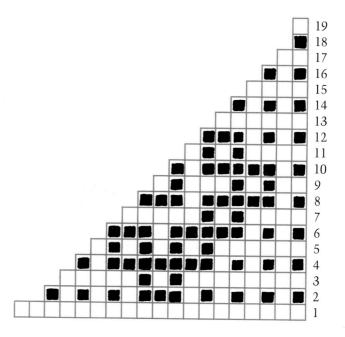

DESIGNING NOTES

The designs for garments and other articles shown in this book are not meant to be copied exactly; they are meant to serve as inspiration, and to give you some stimulating ideas about the kinds of things that can be done with mosaic knitting. Detailed directions for specific garments would be useless to most readers anyway, since it is unlikely that any particular reader would be working with the same combination of yarn type, needle size, stitch gauge, style preference, and body size as the author's. However, detailed directions for working all the basic styles shown in this book in *your own* stitch gauge and size are given in another book, *Knitting from the Top*; and you may also create original mosaic-patterned garments by following commercial pattern directions that match your stitch gauge, or by working to your own measurements.

The following brief outlines of methods, references, colors, and other details are intended to help you visualize the sample designs more precisely, so that you can vary them to suit your own taste and create your own one-of-a-kind fashions. The fundamental purpose of presenting a new technique like mosaic knitting is to set you free from the monotony of "plain knitting" and to show you how easy it is to branch out into excitingly different directions that can refresh your interest in the craft. These outlines are here for you to use if you need them. But don't feel that you *must* use them. Do your own thing, and make your own mosaic designs in your own way; learn the satisfaction of knowing that what you have made is all your own. Happy knitting!

Color 2, sampler-square afghan.

This afghan is worked in Mosaics 9, 13, 14, 19, 37, 38, 40, 42, 45, 47–49, 51–53, 80, 84, 87, 101, 102, 104, 107, and 109; Bands 29, 31, 32, and 34–39; Shadows 1, 14–16, 38, 40, 42–44, 49, 56, 57, 59, 62, and 65. Each square is 51 stitches wide by 102 rows high. The narrow edging is worked in single crochet with an ombre yarn.

Color 5, increased poncho with coordinated pants.

Shaping directions for pants: Reversible Pants (*Knitting from the Top*, p. 62). Additional information on shaping capes and ponchos in general: Seamless Cape (*Knitting from the Top*, pp. 51–54).

Color 6, three sweaters worked in Shadows 9, 29, and 51.

Shaping directions for red, blue, and beige sweater: Square-Set or Peasant Sleeve; for orange, turquoise, and black sweater: Dropped-Shoulder Ski Sweater; for white, navy, and green sweater: Classic Raglan Cardigan, V-neck variation (*Knitting from the Top*, pp. 97, 101, and 36).

Color 7, scrap-yarn coat worked in 26 shadow patterns.

Shaping directions: Seamless Set-In Sleeve, simultaneous method (*Knitting from the Top*, pp. 81–85). Lower portion of this seamless coat is slightly flared with increases evenly spaced in the plain knit rows between patterns, as for a banded skirt.

Color 8, scrap-yarn jacket banded with mosaic designs.

Shaping directions: Square-Set or Peasant Sleeve (*Knitting from the Top*, p. 97). Patterns of this garment include: Pin Check, Stripe and Spot, Honeycomb Tweed, Bricks, Zigzag Checks, Chain Stripes, Shadow Box, Embroidery Check, Beaded Stripe, Sanquar Check (*A Treasury of Knitting Patterns*, pp. 54, 56, 57, 62, 64, 66, 71, 84, and 89); Chessboard, Sliding Block, Basic Fretted Band, Alternating Fretted Band, Assyrian Stripe, Egyptian Cross, Greek Cross Medallion, Fancy Parallelogram, Divided Diamond, Alternating Chain (*A Second Treasury of Knitting Patterns*, pp. 63, 65, 68, 70, 73, 76, 78, 81, and 332); Alternating Key, Shamrock (*Charted Knitting Designs*, pp. 204 and 211).

Color 9, sleeveless blouse and long vest.

Shaping directions for both garments: Sleeveless Sweater (*Knitting from the Top*, p. 71). Patterns of the vest include: Shadow 4 from this volume; Oblong Medallion, Crown Chevron (*A Second Treasury of Knitting Patterns*, pp. 77 and 79); Four-Armed Square, Chevron and Pendants, Wallpaper Lattice, Syncopation I (*Charted Knitting Designs*, pp. 193, 213, 218, and 223); Mosaics 1, 11, 17, 37, 40, 41 (*Sampler Knitting*, pp. 33, 35, 40, 58, and 61).

Figure 74, Mosaic 110 worked in a table mat with a border of Band 81.

After completion of the central pattern square, a 16" circular needle is used to pick up stitches around all 4 edges of the border, which is finished in rounds with seamless increasing corners as for Place Mats.

Figure 75, sampler of Bands 1–13.

This is one-half of the two-strip poncho shown in Figure 159. Colors: black and white.

Figure 76, seamless skirt worked in 13 band patterns.

Borders are plain garter stitch, waistband backed with elastic. Colors: beige and dark brown.

Figure 158, straight-strip pillow cover worked in Mosaic 86.

An ordinary bed pillow covered with mosaic-patterned fabric to double as a sofa cushion. Colors: pale blue and burgundy.

Figure 160, sampler-square afghan.

This afghan is worked the same way as the scrap-yarn afghan shown in Color 2, but with entirely different patterns, and without a crocheted border. Colors: jewel tones (ruby, sapphire, emerald) on white.

Figure 161, sampler-square poncho.

24 afghan squares (5 on each side edge) are joined together to make this basic garment. Fringe strands are knotted on separately, 1 doubled strand to each stitch and side-edge row. Colors: assorted dark tones on white.

Figures 163, 164, and 165, unplanned bias reversible sweaters.

Additional shaping information for garments of this style: Dropped-Shoulder Ski Sweater (*Knitting from the Top*, p. 101). Colors: red, rust, dark brown, and purple on white. Double-bias sweater has plain garter-stitch bands in bright orange, worked on picked-up stitches at borders, shoulder seams, and armhole edges.

Figures 166 and 167, double-bias coat.

Shaping directions: Square-Set or Peasant Sleeve (*Knitting from the Top*, p. 97). Following the basic shape for this style, double-bias back and bias fronts are worked from the top down, with stitches added at underarm level by increasing side edges every other row until the correct width is reached. Sleeves are picked up from armhole edges and worked straight, in the standard manner for this design. Lower portion of coat is slightly flared with increases evenly spaced in plain rows between patterns. Colors: gold, pale green, and white on black.

Figure 168, two mosaic tabards.

Unshaped garment worked in pastel colors with black. Shaped garment worked in Mosaic 22 from *Sampler Knitting* (p. 45) in white, black, and red alternating by Shadow Method III, multicolor reversal. Edges finished with single crochet.

Figures 176 and 178, seamless counterchanged sweaters.

Shaping directions for both garments: Classic Raglan Pullover, reversible boat neckline variation (*Knitting from the Top*, pp. 19–32). Plain garter-stitch borders. Colors for horizontally counterchanged sweater: navy blue and lime green; for vertically counterchanged sweater: black and gold.

Figures 179 and 180, seamless counterchanged jacket worked in Mosaic 53.

Shaping directions: Seamless Set-In Sleeve, simultaneous method (*Knitting from the Top*, pp. 81–85). Narrow borders are made of 2 rows of plain garter stitch firmly bound off. Colors: pale yellow and black.

Figures 181 and 182, counterchanged coat worked in 12 shadow patterns.

Shaping directions: Square-Set or Peasant Sleeve (*Knitting from the Top*, p. 97). Borders are worked in close stitch (*A Treasury of Knitting Patterns*, p. 94). Colors: black and white on red.

Figure 184, two-piece dress trimmed with Shadow 4.

Shaping directions: Seamless Skirt, Seamless Saddle Shoulder (*Knitting from the Top*, pp. 55 and 86). Fabric pattern is a variation of Zigzag Ribbon Stitch, with Picot Hem to finish the skirt (*A Second Treasury of Knitting Patterns*, pp. 123 and 342). Armhole bands are formed by working mosaic trim in the first few sleeve rows after picking up stitches around the armhole. Colors: rose pink with black and silver trim.

Figure 185, tunic-and-pants set with mosaic trim.

Shaping directions: Classic Raglan Pullover, Reversible Pants (*Knitting from the Top*, pp. 19 and 62). Fabric pattern is a variation of Diamond Brocade (*A Treasury of Knitting Patterns*, p. 30). Colors: dark green with chartreuse trim.

Figure 186, sleeveless V-neck pullover.

Shaping directions: Sleeveless Sweater (*Knitting from the Top*, p. 71). Colors: wine and cream.

Figure 187, lace-patterned jacket with mosaic trim.

Shaping directions: Classic Raglan Cardigan (*Knitting from the Top*, p. 36). Colors: white with black and metallic green trim.

Figure 188, seamless pullover worked in Shadow 60.

Shaping directions: Classic Raglan Pullover (*Knitting from the Top*, p. 19). Borders are worked in plain k2, p2 ribbing. Colors: white, powder blue, and navy.

Figure 189, wraparound jackets.

Shaping directions: Dropped-Shoulder Ski Sweater with overlapping kimono front (*Knitting from the Top*, pp. 95, 101). Borders are worked in reverse stockinette (purl side out). Colors: man's jacket—black, brown, and white; boy's jacket—royal blue, blue-gray, and white.

Figure 190, seamless one-piece dress.

Shaping directions: Sleeveless Sweater, reversible boat neckline variation (*Knitting from the Top*, pp. 71–79). Lower portion of the dress is flared with increases evenly spaced between pattern bands. Colors: white, beige, orchid, and chartreuse on black.

Figure 191, V-neck cardigan in 6 shadow patterns.

Shaping directions: Classic Raglan Cardigan, V-neck variation (*Knitting from the Top*, pp. 36–49). All patterns are centered and matched across front and raglan lines. Borders are plain garter stitch, with the back of the neck raised by short rows into a narrow rolled collar. Colors: white, emerald, and navy

Figures 192, 193, and 194, seamless two-piece suits
(skirts, Figures 173, 174, and 175).

Shaping directions for all three outfits: Classic Raglan Cardigan, Seamless Skirt (*Knitting from the Top*, pp. 36 and 55). Patterns of Figure 192 include: Bands 28, 40, and 43 from this volume; Pyramid, Oblong Medallion, Broken Arrow (*A Second Treasury of Knitting Patterns*, pp. 74, 77, and 335); Four-Armed Square, Butterflies, Tilted Swastika and Vine, Chevron and Pendants, Wallpaper Lattice (*Charted Knitting Designs*, pp. 199, 211, 213, and 218); Mosaics 3, 21, 38, and 39 (*Sampler Knitting*, pp. 33, 44, 59, and 60). Colors: red and beige on black. Borders of Figure 193 are worked in garter-stitch variation of Honeycomb Tweed (*A Treasury of Knitting Patterns*, p. 57). Colors: spring green and chocolate brown on white. Borders of Figure 194 are worked in Seed

Stitch (*A Treasury of Knitting Patterns*, p. 11). Colors: orchid and white on deep purple.

Figure 195, seamless jacket in 9 band patterns.

Shaping directions: Seamless Set-In Sleeve, simultaneous method (*Knitting from the Top*, pp. 81–85). Colors: beige and dark brown, to match skirt shown in Figure 76.